EDUARDO MOGA  aw and a PhD in Spanish Philology. He has published 18 poetry collections, the main (1996), *Las horas y los labios* (2003), *Cuerpo sin mí* (2007), *Bajo la piel, los días* (2010), *Insumisión* (2013), *El corazón, la nada (Antología poética 1994-2014)* (2014) and *Muerte y amapolas en Alexandra Avenue* (2017). His poetry has been translated into English (*Selected Poems*, Shearsman Books, 2017), Portuguese, French, Catalan, Italian, Czech, Slovak, Polish, Ukrainian and Albanian. He has translated Ramon Llull, Frank O'Hara, Évariste Parny, Charles Bukowski, Carl Sandburg, Arthur Rimbaud, William Faulkner, Walt Whitman, Richard Aldington and Jaume Roig, among other authors. He currently writes as a literary critic for *Letras Libres, Cuadernos Hispanoamericanos, Turia* and *Quimera*, among other cultural media. He is responsible for the anthologies *Los versos satíricos. Antología de poesía satírica universal* (2001), *Poesía pasión. Doce jóvenes poetas españoles* (2004) and *Medio siglo de oro. Antología de la poesía contemporánea en catalán* (2014). He has also published travel books, such as *La pasión de escribir* (2013) and *El mundo es ancho y diverso* (2018); two selections of posts from his blog *Corónicas de Ingalaterra* (2015 and 2016), where he gathers his impressions of the two years and a half that he lived in London and, in general, of British society; and several volumes of essays, the most recent ones being *La disección de la rosa* (2015), *Apuntes de un español sobre poetas de América (y algunos de otros sitios)* (2016) and *Homo legens* (2018). He has been director of the *Editora Regional de Extremadura* and coordinator of the Reading Promotion Plan of Extremadura. He maintains the blogs *Corónicas de Ingalaterra* and *Corónicas de España*.

TERENCE DOOLEY is currently putting the finishing touches to an anthology of contemporary Spanish women poets for Shearsman. Previous translations include *The Year of the Crab* by Mariano Peyrou, and *Selected Poems* by Eduardo Moga.

STREETS WHERE TO WALK IS TO EMBARK

Spanish Poets in London
(1811-2018)

edited by
Eduardo Moga

translated by
Terence Dooley

Shearsman Books

First published in the United Kingdom in 2019 by
Shearsman Books
50 Westons Hill Drive
Emersons Green
BRISTOL
BS16 7DF

www.shearsman.com

ISBN 978-1-84861-680-6

Introduction and selection copyright © Eduardo Moga, 2019
Translation copyright © Terence Dooley, 2019

All poems reprinted here are copyright © by their respective authors
and publishers, as listed in the 'Sources' on pp. 256-258, except
where specified otherwise below.

The poem by Luis Cernuda is from the book *Las Nubes,* sección VII,
in *La Realidad y el Deseo (1924-1962)* copyright © Herederos de Luis Cernuda
Reprinted with permission.

Poems by Leopoldo María Panero and Juan Luis Panero are
copyright © Herederos de Leopoldo María Panero, and
copyright © Herederos de Juan Luis Panero.

In the cases of José María Aguirre Ruiz
and Pedro Basterra (José García Pradas)
we have been unable to trace the copyright-holders and
the publisher would be pleased to hear from anyone
who controls their literary estates.

INDEX OF AUTHORS

Francisco Martínez de la Rosa	24
Domingo María Ruiz de la Vega	28
José de Espronceda	32
José Alcalá Galiano	42
Miguel de Unamuno	44
José Antonio Balbontín	48
Luis Cernuda	52
Luis Gabriel Portillo	56
Basilio Fernández	58
Pedro Basterra (José García Pradas)	62
José María Aguirre Ruiz	68
Manuel Padorno	70
Rafael Guillén	78
Carlos Sahagún	82
Juan Antonio Masoliver Ródenas	84
Juan Luis Panero	86
Pere Gimferrer	90
Guillermo Carnero	92
Leopoldo María Panero	96
Rafael Argullol	102
Efi Cubero	104
Joaquín Sabina	108
Luis Suñén	112
Ángeles Mora	114
Javier Viriato	116
Javier Pérez Walias	120
Carlos Marzal	124
Eduardo Moga	126
Manuel Vilas	140
Juan Carlos Marset	142
Antonio Rivero Taravillo	154
Balbina Prior	158
Javier Sánchez Menéndez	160
Melchor López	162
Antonio Orihuela	164
Juan Luis Calbarro	174

Juan Carlos Elijas	178
Susana Medina	184
David Torres	188
Jordi Doce	198
Anxo Carracedo	200
Francisco León	204
Julio Mas Alcaraz	206
Mercedes Cebrián	212
Óscar Curieses	218
Teresa Guzmán	222
Ernesto García López	224
Antonio Reseco	236
José Luis Rey	240
Ignacio Cartagena	244
José Manuel Díez	246
José Daniel García	248
Mario Martín Gijón	250
Jèssica Pujol	252
María Salvador	254
Sources of the poems	256

FOREWORD

Londres es todo niebla y gente triste.
No sé si es la niebla la que produce la gente triste,
o si es la gente triste la que produce la niebla.
OSCAR WILDE

London is too full of fogs and serious people.
Whether the fogs produce the serious people,
or whether the serious people produce the fogs, I don't know.
OSCAR WILDE

For centuries London was the capital of the world, and it remains, even today, one of the most fascinating cities in the world, a magnet for writers intrigued by its diversity and contradictions. Before the 19th century, very few Spaniards had seen or written about it, although there was perhaps an early missed opportunity. Fernando Sánchez de Tovar, an admiral in the service of Enrique II and Juan I of Castile, sailed up the Thames in 1380, in the middle of the Hundred Years' War, with the wicked aim of sacking London, having already twice laid waste to the main South coast ports from Plymouth to Folkestone, but he got no further than Gravesend, which, either from habit or from frustration at not having reached the capital, he razed to the ground. This feat of the devastating admiral is fittingly described by Pedro López de Ayala in the *Crónicas de los reyes de Castilla* [*Chronicles of the Kings of Castile*] devoted to Juan I: 'They waged great war on the seas in this year, and sailed up the Artemis (Thames) further than any enemy galleons had reached, almost as far as London'. Though, even had Sánchez de Tovar reached London, it's extremely improbable he would have left us his written impressions: he'd have been too busy burning the place down.

Not until long after those troubled times do we encounter a significant presence of Spanish writers in England. In the reign of Elizabeth II, London became the refuge of choice for exiled Spanish Protestants. The three most important were Casiodoro de Reina, Cipriano de Valera, and Antonio del Corro. De Reina translated the first full version of the Bible in Spanish, the *Biblia del oso* [*Bear Bible*], published in Basel in 1569, which de Valera later corrected as the *Biblia del cántaro* [*Jug Bible*] in 1602. Now known as the *Biblia Reina-Valera*, this is the most beautiful of all the translations into Spanish. Antonio del Corro, an Oxford don, wrote the first Spanish grammar for English use, published in 1590, as an introduction to the first Spanish-English dictionary. In the reign of James I, another protestant priest, Juan de Luna, wrote the extremely anticlerical *Segunda parte de la vida de Lazarillo de Tormes* [*Second Part of the Life of Lazarillo de Tormes*], which was published in Paris in 1620, an English translation following in 1622. In 1623 he published a new edition in English and Spanish of his Spanish textbook *Arte breve y compendioso para aprender a leer, pronunciar, escribir y hablar la lengua española* [*Brief and Compendious Art of Learning to Read, Pronounce, Write and Speak the Spanish Tongue*], which had been a success in France as a Spanish text in 1615. None of these writers, however, or any other of the Spanish Protestants who sought refuge here during the period, left a written record of their life in the British Isles, perhaps because of their struggle to earn a living. For Casiodoro de Reina, there was the added complication of his having to face accusations of being a spy in the service of Elizabeth I, and a practising homosexual.

The first account of a Spanish writer's experiences in London is the poet and playwright Leandro Fernández de Moratín's *Apuntaciones sueltas de Inglaterra* [*Notes on England*],[1] which remained unpublished until 1984. Moratín had been given a grant by the government of Manuel Godoy to study French theatre in Paris, but in 1792 he fled the horrors of the guillotine to study English theatre in London, where he stayed a year. He became the first translator of *Hamlet* directly from the English, in 1798, and wrote poems about British heroes such as Nelson. *Notes on England* is a delight: a mélange of diary, essay and travel-writing in which he relates what he sees in late 18th century London in a highly lively style, a mixture of wit, astonishment and the scientific spirit. He memorably lists the 'implements, devices and instruments needed to serve tea to two guests in any decent English home', twenty-four in total. Also memorable are his reflections on religious freedom; Englishwomen's feet ('enormous'); suicide ('very common in England: the people's melancholy nature is exacerbated by their environment and, after due consideration, they resolve that they should kill themselves'); the clergy – 'canons, deans, archdeacons and bishops' – who stroll arm in arm with their wives and surrounded by their children; the kangaroo, that animal 'newly discovered (…), tranquil and well-mannered'; donkeys, 'of greater utility and better treated than in Madrid', because, instead of bearing loads of plaster, brick and stone on their backs, with the consequent risk of collapse under the weight, they pull it along behind them in carts; ostentatious funerals, because 'in England much attention is lavished on the dead'; and, finally, his half-amazed, half-revolted depiction of the English passion for alcohol:

> 'The Prince of Wales is drunk every night: drunkenness is not considered a vice in England, and it's the most usual thing in the world to encounter distinguished persons four sheets to the wind in private houses, pubs and theatres. When a foreigner is a guest at an English table, he must either get drunk with everyone else, or lose the good opinion of his host, and the company; he may not abstain or drink moderately. No excuse is accepted; any refusal is an affront, an unforgiveable insult. As soon as the tablecloths are removed, the bottles arrive and the toasts begin; with each toast a glass of wine must be drunk. The first toast is generally to His Majesty and our glorious Constitution; then every single person present toasts someone dear to him, an absent friend, and everyone drinks, repeating the toast, and all this is performed with a ceremony and gravity ridiculous to behold, and so on, from toast to toast, so that everyone must drink as many glasses as there are people invited. And after the first round there is usually a second or third, and there they sit for four, six, eight hours not moving from the table except to urinate, which they do in a large bucket placed for that purpose in a corner of the room'.

Almost a century later, Benito Pérez Galdós, one of the greatest 19th century European novelists, visited England three times, in 1883, 1886 and 1889, to survey in detail the London described by Dickens, his idol. During his third visit he also went to Stratford, and around 1895 he published *La casa de Shakespeare* [*Shakespeare's House*],[2] in which he writes about the absence of Spanish names in the visitor's book: 'I believe I am one of the very few, perhaps the only Spaniard to have visited that literary Jerusalem and I confess I am proud to have rendered this homage to the most sublime of all poets…'. Of London, however, he gives a less flattering picture, focusing on those left on the margins of the prosperity brought by capitalism:

> 'In the very centre of the city, around the hotels and train stations, one sees flocks of ragged children, with sooty faces and bare feet, and without shelter of any kind. It's dreadful to think of these poor creatures' existence when winter's rigours set in'.

In 1905, *Los ingleses vistos por un latino: impresiones de viaje* [*The English as Seen by a Latin: Travel Notes*]³ by the Catalan Federico Rahola Trèmols, a little-known writer in comparison with those mentioned above, saw the light of day. Rahola depicts Albion favourably and admiringly, but not without irony. Unsurprisingly, when we think of Moratín, his first chapter is called *Alcohol in England:*

> 'In England, to get drunk is the most natural thing in the world, as natural as it is for us to bask in the winter sunshine back home. It's the only way the English have to leave their island without crossing the channel. The flecks of soot in the air, the constant roar of machinery, the black-stained buildings, the thick and penetrating fog, the gloomy expressions and the shut mouths form an entity driving them to drink, as we are drawn to light'.

Also like Moratín, Rahola dwells unflatteringly on the Englishwoman's feet: 'Her face is a poem and her feet monstrous; one's eyes skip from Greek sculpture to grotesque late Baroque; an angel would be happy with her countenance and a clodhopper disdain her soles. It's as if an exquisite form were placed on a pedestal of disproportionate size', though, in a footnote, he has the grace to admit: 'This isn't always the case'.

Pío Baroja, another great Spanish novelist and Dickens devotee, like Galdós, came first to London in 1906 to explore the Dickensian city. After a month of tramping its streets, he realised, as he writes in his memoirs, that it was a world even wider than his hero's novels, 'impossible to understand given many months or years; a world wrapped in darkness and fog, of unfeasible distances, with a greater gulf fixed between extreme wealth and abject poverty than anywhere else'. This first stay gave rise to his novel of 1909 *La ciudad de la niebla* [*The City of Fog*],⁴ set entirely in London, which depicts scenes of misery and lowlife similar to those described by Galdós.

> 'At nightfall, these streets around Covent Garden market became lively: overweight women, scruffy girls and a swarm of little ragamuffins emerged from the doorways. These children did not seem light-hearted and gay like poor children in Spain: they were dirty, miserable; the girls looked squashed by huge woollen berets; the boys, shy and quiet, hardly played. (…). From every house and tavern came the sound of rows and fighting. Men beat their wives and children mercilessly. It was wretched to see, in the midst of a

civilisation so perfect in so many other ways, that children were treated more cruelly here than anywhere else in the world'.

Baroja came again to England in the middle of the Spanish Civil War, and stayed from 1937 to 1939. This time he also travelled outside London. The city plays a central role in several novels inspired by this second visit: *Los impostores joviales* [*Jovial Imposters*], *Laura o La soledad sin remedio* [*Laura or Incurable Loneliness*], *Los espectros del castillo* [*The Castle Ghosts*], and *El hotel del cisne* [*The Swan Hotel*].

In 1916, the Galician writer and journalist, Julio Camba, published an extraordinary collection, simply titled *Londres. Impresiones de un español* [*London. A Spaniard's Impressions*].[5] He arrived in London at the end of 1910 as correspondent to the newspaper *El Mundo,* and, in the course of a long year's stay, wrote more than 150 articles which appeared in the Spanish press over the next two years. Then he returned to England in 1913, this time for only a few months. Taken together, the articles which make up *London...* form one of the most intelligent and good-humoured portraits ever painted of the city. Camba writes with the same mild irony and subtle pungency employed by the British in their travels abroad, perhaps because, as a Galician, he like them had come under a Celtic influence. The humour in this light-hearted book arises from the perpetual contrast between Camba's mañana-ism, spontaneity and sense of fun, and the puritanism of his hosts, determined to observe the law, pay bills on time, and suffer the rain. Despite his originality of tone, the reader will recognise certain topics from previous travellers' chronicles. For example, Camba discusses 'English suicide' like Moratín; sandwich-men like Rahola; and the Englishwoman's feet, like both of them ('she has big feet so as not to fall over'). Also, predictably, drunkenness, and the food, dull and unappetising (Camba was a gourmet, and wrote one of the best books on gastronomy of the 20th century, *La casa de Lúculo* [*The House of Lucullus*]), the fog and the rain. In the memorable first article in *London...,* *El guardia objetivamente considerado* [*An Objective Look at the Police*], he takes the 'bobby' as a metaphor for the unblinking imperturbability of the society in which he finds himself.

> 'There seems to me something superhuman about the English policeman; he is above our passions and everyday sentiments. Once I had to ask one the way; I approached him and gazed up at him. The policeman had his head in the air and didn't see me. I called to him, to ask my question. Then the policemen, without

looking in my direction, gave me a most detailed answer and, as I went on my way, he still held his impassive statuesque pose. And this is because when you ask an English policeman a question it's not you he answers, he is answering society. Whether you are well or badly dressed and whether you're polite or rude won't influence his response. I already said he was superhuman. His spirit is the spirit of duty. If you or I or anyone approaches him, we are society calling. The policeman answers, that is all'.

The first Spanish poets to write about London arrived in the city in the most substantial of the many political migrations of the 19th century. Ferdinand VII twice declared absolute power (in 1814 and in 1823) and Romantics and liberals fled his persecutions. A thousand or more Spanish families set up home in the capital, most of them in Somers Town, near King's Cross, which became the quintessential Spanish *barrio*. England became their destination, since no other country (all of them ruled by the heirs of the *ancien régime*) would accept the Spanish revolutionaries, but the United Kingdom still gave shelter to the oppressed and believed in free thought and free expression. Valentín Llanos Gutiérrez, a friend of Keats who wrote novels in English, expresses this well: England was 'the only country in Europe where the honourable patriot could find a refuge and a sympathetic welcome, and breathe the health-giving air of liberty'. Among those refugees were well-known literary figures such as José Joaquín de Mora, journalist and poet, translator of Walter Scott and Jeremy Bentham; Bartolomé José Gallardo, poet and satirist, literary critic, bibliophile and serial book-thief, who composed, while in London, *El panteón de El Escorial* [*The Escorial Pantheon*], a violent and factual poetic diatribe against all the Spanish kings, from the *Reyes Católicos* to the vile Ferdinand VII himself; Ángel de Saavedra, Duke of Rivas, poet and author of the classic Romantic drama *Don Álvaro o La fuerza del sino* [*Don Álvaro or The Force of Destiny*], which until recently all Spanish children studied for the Baccalaureate; Antonio Alcalá Galiano, who lived in England for many years and, despite his dire need, refused a British government grant, because he was writing a biography of Rafael del Riego which criticised that government's treatment of him, and who also became the first Professor of Spanish at London University; and José de Espronceda, poet and standard-bearer for Spanish Romanticism who lived in London from 1827 to 1829, and again in 1832. As well as pursuing their own work, many of them contributed to the reviews or magazines published by the Spanish colony. The most significant of these, perhaps, was *Ocio de*

Españoles Emigrados [*Entertainment for Spanish Migrants*], which ran from 1824 to 1827.⁶ A series of articles by an anonymous contributor, 'The Migrant', gives us a splendid picture, not only of pre-Victorian London but also of the Spanish mindset in those years. 'The Migrant' is first of all amazed at the traffic, 'the vast agglomerations of people, which lead to collisions and fracas, without the consolation of being able to give the perpetrator a good mouthful, since he wouldn't understand us, it would be like preaching in the desert'. He praises the 'peerless nocturnal illumination, provided by the happy invention of gas', and his admiration is understandable, given that gaslight didn't reach Spain until 1841. He has interesting things to say about men and women's clothing: the men don't wear shorts, but 'trousers and tailcoats –even the road-sweepers'. But the way the women dress raises a difficulty: 'Though they dress with utmost decency, the way their corsets emphasise the figure arouses violent passions in us Spaniards'. Imagine the torture these Catholic Spanish exiles endured, strolling around London and witnessing those balconied bosoms. He also notes the effects of Spanish clothes on the English: 'I'm surprised to see that our capes are more ridiculous to them than Greek or Asiatic costume. What would they say if they saw someone in Maragato or Valencian costume? And are these more shocking than a Scotsman in his kilt?'. But these Spanish capes brought insults as well as mockery: 'They called us French dogs (…). But, when we told them we were Spanish, they began to praise us instead, for these people know full well that our resistance, loyalty and honour halted Napoleon in his tracks and put an end to the threat to their might and well-being'. These exiles so disconcerted by Englishwomen's figures, being used to Spanish women shrouded in layers of clothing, are also disconcerted by their behaviour: they go out alone, and no-one shouts compliments after them. So, 'such is the general law abidingness, young girls leave their houses unaccompanied and travel by coach from one town to another'. And he gives an admiring example: 'A girl, a gentleman's daughter, was in the carriage with us all the way from Bristol to London'. Though he doesn't mention her feet.

Setting aside the chronicles of 'The Migrant', which one may consider an exception, few other exiles paid much attention to their host city during their stay, nor did they view it with affection. They were sunk in melancholy: their main preoccupation was getting back to a Spain which they felt to be suffering in darkness. Even their poems about London, such as those by Espronceda and Martínez de la Rosa in this anthology, are really about Spain: transpositions of a more desired place. The Duke de Rivas wrote poems with eloquent titles such as *El desterrado* [*The Outcast*] and *El sueño del proscrito* [*The Outlaw's Dream*]. In the latter he writes:

> I wake with a start
> and find myself a fugitive
> from Spanish soil,
> the place of my birth (…);
> and instead of the balm
> of the soft breeze
> of the Andalusian sky
> which I loved so,
> the foul fogs
> of the frigid Thames
> sick at heart
> shall I inhale…

A forerunner of these writers was the unusual and eminent figure José María Blanco White, who set up home in England in 1810, fleeing the Bonapartist Spanish government, and never returned to Spain, dying in Liverpool in 1841. He was atypical in that he wrote in English. Among his works are the memorable *Letters from Spain* and the sonnet *Night and Death*, described by Coleridge as 'the finest and most grandly conceived sonnet in our language'.

A second wave of poets and writers arrived in the United Kingdom during the Spanish Civil War or after the Republic's fall, in 1939. The best-known were Luis Cernuda, Pedro Garfias, Arturo Barea, Esteban Salazar Chapela, Manuel Chaves Nogales and José Antonio Balbontín. Cernuda, an Andalusian from Seville, lived in Great Britain from 1938 to 1947: in Glasgow, in Cambridge and in London. His years of exile were a torment to him: the weather, the puritanism and coldness of the people, a thriving capitalism deadly to the imagination and to *joie de vivre*. If London suffocated him with its crowds and tumult, Glasgow was even more hellish, a frigid inferno, although early on he discovered the 'morning delight of bathing with *déshabillés* or naked Scotsmen'. But he found the Caledonian city dark, soporific, desolate: a 'heap of management niches', 'a sink'. In 1943 he moved to Cambridge, where he taught Spanish at Emmanuel College. This was the high point of Cernuda's time in England: he was at least contented there; one could never say he was truly happy anywhere. Finally, in 1945, he went to work in London, at the Spanish Institute, which was financed by the Republican government in exile, and began to write literary criticism for the *Bulletin of Hispanic Studies*. He spent his summers in Oxford with his friend the painter Gregorio Prieto. Though he didn't enjoy himself much in England, his stay greatly benefited his writing: he read the Metaphysical poets, Eliot, Auden, Wordsworth, Blake, Yeats, Shelley, Keats and Browning, and translated Shakespeare's *Troilus and Cressida*. All this reading (as he explains in *Historial de un libro* [*History of a book*]) led Cernuda to reject the pathetic fallacy and excessive aestheticism, and to develop an elegant plain style. The subtlety and naturalness so characteristic of English literature would be evident in his writing for the rest of his life, and would exert a profound influence on Spanish poets up to the present day. He had good words too to say about his fellow countrymen of the past decade, with whom he had suffered the horrors of the Second World War: 'The English, for me at least, don't inspire warm feelings, but I can't think of a people I admire or respect more'. And elsewhere: 'England is the most civilized country I know of, the place where civilisation has reached its apogee. All one can do is bow to its superiority and learn from it, or leave'. He decided to leave, and was glad to go. We see this in his poem *La partida* [*Leaving*], written in America. It details his impressions of grey rivers, damp skies, all he had to live through, and it ends prophetically: 'Farewell cold land, cold as your men,/ Where error took me and where error bids me leave./ Thanks for everything and thanks for nothing./ I won't be back again'.

Another Andalusian, Pedro Garfias, only spent a few months in England, but started on the road to alcoholism there, and wrote *Primavera en Eaton Hastings (Poema bucólico con intermedios de llanto)* [*Spring in Eaton Hastings (Pastoral with Interludes of Lament)*],[7] which he published on his arrival in Mexico, in June 1939, which Dámaso Alonso described as the best of all poems about Spanish exile. He wrote it in the village of the same name, home of Alexander Gavin Henderson, 2nd Baron Faringdon, a Labour peer who had given him shelter. *Spring in Eaton Hastings* takes up again that song for Spain sung by the exiled liberals of the early 19th century. In the interlude *Noche con estrellas* [*Starry Night*] he writes:

> Although, frail dome, you crack, this starry night,
> into a thousand shards,
> I must cry out amid this English wood
> of thoughtful oaks and lofty, sounding pines.
> I must uproot the trees convulsively,
> and batter on the heavens with my fists,

and weep out loud this bitten misery
that wells and gushes from my inmost self.

Alone amid a race who shape their fate
and roll their dice with calculating eye;
who work and play and take their Sunday rest
and all week long patrol their vast estates,
as vigilant as sheepdog with its herd;
who walk straight paths as one parts children's hair;
who gobble the black entrails of their soil
with a green tongue of parterres and of parks;
who tend their flowers with a Franciscan care,
who tend their fish and birds and enslave India;
alone amid a race who sleep tonight
alone I shed my tears.

Although the silence creak, the swan awake
(that Royal swan) and break the quiet waters
with its wings; although the waters flow
and softly tap their knuckles on the bank
and the din spread throughout the listening wood
and finally awake the sleeping breeze
behind the curve of hill; though the breeze swoop
to shake the meadows, rattle window-panes;
although the quivering note should reach the stars,
perturb the constellations in their seat
while England sleeps, I bellow my lament
like a poor calf who's from his mother rent.

Though Garfias wasn't in England long, his stay did include an extraordinary episode recounted by Pablo Neruda in *Confieso que he vivido* [*Memoirs*],[8] a kind of metaphor for communication between people and, by extension, peoples. Neruda writes:

> '(Garfias) went to stay in the castle of a lord (...). He was always by himself there and, as he was a restless Andalusian, he would go every day to the village pub and silently (since he couldn't speak English, only a gypsified Spanish which I could barely understand myself) drink a depressed and solitary beer. The publican was much intrigued by this mute customer. One night, when all

the other drinkers had gone home, he invited him to stay behind and the two of them went on drinking by the fire, whose crackling did the talking for them.

This invitation became a ritual. Every night Garfias was welcomed by the publican, who was also lonely, with no wife or family. Gradually their tongues were loosened. Garfias told him the whole story of the Civil War, with exclamations, oaths and Andalusian curses. The innkeeper heard him out in devoted silence, naturally not understanding a single word.

Then the Scotsman began to relate his own misfortunes, probably how his wife had left him (…). I say probably because, in all the long months of these bizarre exchanges, Garfías didn't understand a single word either.

Nonetheless, the friendship of the two lonely men, each speaking passionately of his own concerns and in his own language, unintelligible to the other, grew and grew: to meet every night and talk till dawn became a necessity to them both.

When Garfias had to leave, to go to Mexico, they bid each other farewell drinking and talking, weeping and embracing. What they both felt so deeply was the parting of their solitudes. *I never understood a word, Pablo, but whenever I listened to him I felt… I was certain I caught the sense of what he was saying. And when I spoke I was sure he understood me too'.*

Arturo Barea, from Extremadura, also fled Spain after the defeat of the Republican forces. He settled in London and worked for the Spanish section of the BBC's World Service from 1940 until his death in 1957. He gave more than 900 talks for them under the pseudonym of Juan de Castilla. He later took British nationality and moved to Eaton Hastings (thanks again to Baron Faringdon) with his wife, the Austrian journalist Ilse Kulcsar. In London he wrote one of the most significant books of 20th century Spanish exile, the novelised autobiography *La forja de un rebelde* [*The Forging of a Rebel*]. Translated by Ilse, it was first published in English in three parts, between 1941 and 1946, and was a great success both in the UK and the US. The first edition in Spanish was published in 1951 in Argentina. Unsurprisingly, given Franco's animus against Barea, whom he called 'the English Beria', this major work didn't come out in Spain until 1977.[9]

José Antonio Balbontín was another defender of the Republic who sought exile in London in 1939, where he lived until 1970, returning then to Spain, where, in 1978, he died. Like many other exiles, he made his living from translation and his meagre royalties. In England he wrote *Por el amor de España y de la Idea. Cien sonetos de combate contra Franco y sus huestes* [*For Love of Spain and the Idea: 100 Fighting Sonnets against Franco and his Hordes*], a ferocious political diatribe which he published in Mexico under the pseudonym Juan de Luz in 1956; and *A la orilla del Támesis (Poemas del destierro)* [*On the Banks of the Thames (Poems of Exile)*], 44 poems expressing the longing for Spain one would expect in a Spanish poet in exile, as well as the misery of London life, and also his admiration for Byron, Shelley and Keats, published in 2005.[10] This wasn't the only one of Balbontín's works to be published long after his death: *Mis impresiones de Inglaterra* [*My Impressions of England*], a prose memoir intended 'to set down plainly, as in a family letter, for friends who may be interested, some of my personal impressions from throughout my exile in England, a country which has been my second homeland, and which I will hold in my memory when I return to my true homeland, where my only dream is to die in peace under the sun of Castile, if God allows me this grace', did not appear until 2013.[11]

Two more writers, who died in exile, should be mentioned. The first, Esteban Salazar Chapela, became Spanish consul for the Republic in Glasgow in 1937. In 1939, he moved to London with his wife and, in 1941, began to work for the BBC World Service, also teaching at Cambridge. He became secretary of the Republican Spanish Institute when it opened in 1944. In 1947, his *Perico en Londres* [*Perico in London*], an idiosyncratic narrative, part humorous, part wistful, was published in Argentina,[12] as well as the light-hearted *Desnudo en Piccadilly* [*Naked in Piccadilly*], in 1959. His *Cartas de Londres* [*Letters from London*], articles in which he commented on the cultural, social and political life of the U.K, and news items on Spanish and Latin American themes, appeared in the principal Latin American newspapers. He died in London in 1965. In *Perico in London* he writes:

> 'Who am I?' (…). 'A Spaniard'. 'What am I doing here in the swaddled island, below pearl-grey skies?'. 'Waiting perhaps'. 'Why am I here? Why aren't I in the Paseo de la Castellana, the Rambla de las Flores or in the María Luisa park?'. 'Because if you showed your face in any of those places you'd be a dead man' (…). 'In that case, I'm a hunted man, what they call a fugitive, who is here on this kindly hospitable island simply because he cannot

be back there' (…). 'What did I do?'. 'You disagreed, in other words you are heterodox, heterodox, Perico'. 'How silly! (…) and just for that they'd kill me if I showed my face in the Paseo de la Castellana, the Rambla de las Flores or in the María Luisa park?' (…). 'Certainly, it's ridiculous, grotesque, but I've seen it happen many times'. 'Where?'. 'In Spain'. 'When?'. 'For the last five centuries' (…). 'From the 16th century to the present day' (…). 'They were heterodox too. But in the 16th and 17th centuries they called them Protestants, and in the 18th century encyclopaedists, and in the 19th century constitutionalists and liberals. Now in the 20th century they're called republicans, although it's true you could call them antifascists, since they are both things'. 'And what became of the heterodox of, the 16th, 17th, 18th and 19th centuries?'. 'All who managed to escape came to this island'. 'To this island? Like me?'. 'Exactly like you'. 'Oh, Perico! What a wonderful and heartbreaking discovery!'. 'As wonderful and heartbreaking as the raging river of our history'. 'Therefore I must have, here on British soil, perhaps on the very greensward of this peaceful park, an army of Spaniards, ghostly, invisible to mortal eyes, keeping me company… That's right, isn't it, Perico, these ghosts are by my side?'. 'They're with you, Perico. They are your ancestors'.

Manuel Chaves Nogales, Andalusian like Cernuda, fled Franco for Paris in 1936, then fled Hitler for London in 1940. He was a well-known journalist and writer of many books, including one of the best books on the Civil War, a collection of nine stories, *A sangre y fuego: héroes, bestias y mártires de España* [*By Blood and Fire: Heroes, Beasts and Martyrs of Spain*], published in Santiago de Chile in 1937. In London he founded and ran *The Atlantic Pacific Press Agency*, was a columnist on the *Evening Standard*, and worked for the BBC World Service, like Barea, Salazar Chapela and many other Republican exiles, before his early death from cancer in 1944.

During the long night of Franco's dictatorship, Spaniards continued to emigrate as they had always done. But few now came to the UK. Latin America, because of the shared language and culture, and a handful of European countries, France, Germany and Switzerland, were the main destinations of a primarily economic, though never without some political motive, migration. Only 5% of Spaniards emigrating within Europe settled in Great Britain. Despite the dictatorship and Spain's isolation, poets and writers continued to visit England, usually to work in academia, as university language or literature teachers. Already, before the Civil War, various members of the celebrated 1927 generation of poets had set an example: Manuel Altolaguirre lived in London from 1933 to 1935, where he founded and edited the bilingual magazine *1616* (the year both Shakespeare and Cervantes died), publishing his own translations of T. S. Eliot and Byron and part of Shelley's *Adonaïs*; Dámaso Alonso taught at Oxford and Cambridge; Jorge Guillén at Oxford; and Pedro Salinas at Cambridge. After the war, other well-known poets followed in their footsteps: Claudio Rodríguez at Nottingham; José Ángel Valente at Oxford; and Juan Antonio Masoliver Ródenas, who became Professor of Spanish and Latin American Studies at the University of Westminster. However, none of them wrote about London, with the exception of Masoliver Ródenas, whose poem is in this anthology. Only in the 1970s, when Franco's dictatorship was loosening its hold, and then in the early years of democracy, did a new wave of young poets arrive in London to enjoy the freedom, cosmopolitan atmosphere, and wealth of culture it offered. This latter group did write about their experiences. Some of them – Gimferrer, Leopoldo María Panero, Carnero – belonged to or moved in the orbit of the *novísimo* group, writing a new poetry no longer rooted in social concerns; others were free spirits, hungry for life and independence, who, as they washed dishes in Soho restaurants or strummed guitars in the underground, soaked up the atmosphere and described it or let it filter through in their stories and poems.

With the coming of democracy and entry into the Common Market, Spain became a modern society, with opportunities to travel to London for the majority, as a tourist or a student – not just, as before, to taste bohemia, to work as an *au pair*, or to procure an abortion. Many people came, up until the 2008 recession, which was especially devastating in Spain because of the collapse of a large part of the financial system and many building societies. This produced an influx of economic migrants to the UK, in search of work or prospects unavailable to them in their own country. At least 200,000 Spaniards now live in Britain, around half of them in London. They are no longer fleeing political repression, but attempting to escape poverty and inequality. And, as they struggle to improve their own lot, and to contribute to the society that welcomes them, some of them write about their experience. So do some of the students, teachers and the many tourists still attracted to a seductive and troubling, tranquil and bewildering, wealthy and mysterious city, where one is never sure if the fog makes people sad, or the sad people make the fog.

This anthology

I bring together in *Streets Where to Walk Is to Embark* a wide selection of poems written about the city over the past two centuries by Spanish poets. The starting date had to be 1800 as I couldn't find anything written earlier.

The poems had to be recognisably about the city. There are probably many more poems written *in* London by Spanish poets, but I wasn't about to enter into an archaeology of creation or sift through biographies, a task beyond the scope of this anthology: I wanted poems that mentioned London, whatever else they were also about. So all these poems have an explicit connection to the city. Sometimes London is the protagonist, sometimes the setting, and sometimes it represents an outside space which the poet interiorises, but it always remains a real place, an urban environment to accept as it is or to confront.

I didn't select the poems on the basis of form or style. *Streets Where to Walk Is to Embark* contains every kind of expression, tradition, sensibility and voice – the only benchmark for inclusion was quality. So the anthology, as well as being a balanced history, is also a display of the breadth of styles of current Spanish poetry, and of the poetry of the past.

The poems had to have been already published. I wasn't looking for new work, but for a significant historical record.

The poets are all Spanish, writing in Spanish, with the sole exception of Jèssica Pujol, who wrote her poem in English. I haven't included poetry in the other peninsular languages, though I know of some poems on London in Catalan and there may be others in Galician or Basque. Many Latin American poets have also written about London, either in Spanish or Portuguese, from the Peruvian Antonio Cisneros to the Brazilian Vinícius de Moraes. So have many Portuguese, such as Alberto Lacerda, Mário Cesariny, and Manuel A. Domingos, and many French, most famously Rimbaud and Verlaine, pursuing their tormented love-affair. In fact London has been a focus for world literature in numerous languages, too many for this anthology to contemplate or to include. So I've confined myself to my mother tongue, the language I write my own poems in, and I believe I've made a representative and generous selection of Spanish poetry which recognises, and pays homage to, the affectionate relationship between our two venerable nations, which has had its ups and downs over the centuries, but which has been so fruitful in terms of mutual literary artistic and social interchange. On other matters: I'm disappointed not to have been able to include more women poets, but I could hardly find any poems about London written by women. And please forgive me for including one of my own poems. I thought that its theme (and I hope quality) justified its presence, but its presence is also my personal homage to a city in which I spent two and a half years of my life, angst-ridden, but also revitalized and hopeful. I miss it more and more.

ACKNOWLEDGEMENTS

My grateful thanks to all those who suggested possible poems for inclusion in this anthology. Also to my translator Terence Dooley, who has generously supported this project from the beginning and who I am proud to call my friend. And many thanks to Tony Frazer, of Shearsman Books, for his support for poetry in Spanish wherever it is written, and for once again so cordially opening his doors to me.

Eduardo Moga
Sant Cugat del Vallès (Barcelona),
December 16th, 2018

PUBLICATION NOTES

[1] The first (incomplete) edition was published in 1984. Many editions followed. The one used here was Ana Rodríguez-Fischer's, Promociones y Publicaciones Universitarias, 1992.
[2] Antonio López, editor, Librería Española; recently reissued: Rey Lear, 2007.
[3] Antonio López, editor, Librería Española.
[4] Bruguera, 1980.
[5] There are modern editions, the most recent by Francisco Fuster García in Reino de Cordelia, 2012.
[6] All editions of the magazine have been scanned and are available online in the Biblioteca Virtual Miguel de Cervantes: http://www.cervantesvirtual.com/portales/ocios_de_espanoles_emigrados/.
[7] The most recent edition was published by Point de Lunettes, 2018.
[8] Seix Barral, 1974. English edition by Penguin, 1978.
[9] Turner. Many further editions followed, notably Gregorio Torres Nebrera's for Editora Regional de Extremadura in 2009. There have also been several English (and American) editions, the most recent by Pushkin Press (2018).
[10] Edition by Aitor L. Larrabide, Ayuntamiento de Santa María de Cayón, colección «La Sirena del Pisueña», nº 23.
[11] Edition by Aitor L. Larrabide, Renacimiento.
[12] Buenos Aires, Losada.

FRANCISCO MARTÍNEZ DE LA ROSA
(Granada, 1787–Madrid, 1862)

EL RECUERDO DE LA PATRIA
(En Londres, año de 1811)

    Vi en el Támesis umbrío
Cien y cien naves cargadas
De riqueza;
Vi su inmenso poderío,
Sus artes tan celebradas,
Su grandeza.
    Mas el ánima afligida
Mil suspiros exhalaba
Y ayes mil;
Y ver la orilla florida
Del manso Dauro anhelaba
Y del Genil.
    Vi de la soberbia corte
Las damas engalanadas,
Muy vistosas;
Vi las bellezas del norte,
De blanca nieve formadas
Y de rosas:
    Sus ojos de azul del cielo;
De oro puro parecía
Su cabello;
Bajo transparente velo
Turgente el seno se vía,
Blanco y bello.
    ¿Mas qué valen los brocados,
Las sedas y pedrería
De la ciudad?
¿Qué los rostros sonrosados,
La blancura y gallardía,
Ni la beldad?
    Con mostrarse mi zagala,
De blanco lino vestida,
Fresca y pura,

FRANCISCO MARTÍNEZ DE LA ROSA

REMEMBRANCE OF HIS HOMELAND
(London, 1811)

   On the umbrous Thames I saw
One hundred and a hundred ships
With riches laden;
I dwelt on its vast power,
Its arts wide-famed,
Its grandeur.
   But my wretched soul
A thousand moans exhaled,
A thousand sighs;
I yearned to gaze upon
Sweet Dauro's flowered shore
And the Gentil.
   I saw great ladies of the court
Bedecked in their proud
Hauteur.
I saw the beauties of the North,
Of white snow made
And roses:
   Their eyes celestial blue;
Their bright hair shining
Pure as gold;
Beneath transparent veil
Their bosoms swell
White and beautiful.
   But what avail
The fine brocade, the silk,
The jewelled city?
And what the blushing skin,
The white, the gallantry,
The beauty?
   When my dear girl appears,
Clothed in white linen,
Cool and pure,

Condena la inútil gala,
Y se esconde confundida
La hermosura.
　　¿Dó hallar en climas helados
Sus negros ojos graciosos,
Que son fuego,
Ora me miren airados,
Ora roben cariñosos
Mi sosiego?
　　¿Dó la negra cabellera
Que al ébano se aventaja?
¿Y el pie leve,
Que al triscar por la pradera,
Ni las tiernas flores aja,
Ni aun las mueve…?
　　Doncellas las del Genil,
Vuestra tez escurecida
No trocara
Por los rostros de marfil
Que Albión envanecida
Me mostrara.
　　Padre Dauro, manso río
De las arenas doradas,
Dígnate oír
Los votos del pecho mío;
¡Y en tus márgenes sagradas
Logre morir!

She banishes vain show,
And modesty conceals
Her loveliness.
   Where in frosty climes to find
The grace of her black eyes
Of fire,
Now may they flash at mine,
Now, doting, steal away
My care?
   Where her black tresses
Finer far than ebony?
And her light foot,
That, tripping through the meadows,
Harms not the wild flowers,
Nor stirs them?
   Oh, damsel of the Gentil,
Your dusk complexion
I would praise
Above all marble
Proud Albion
Displays.
   Father Dauro, sweet river
Of golden sands,
Pray hearken to
My heartfelt cry;
And on your sacred margin
May I die!

DOMINGO MARÍA RUIZ DE LA VEGA
(Seville, 1789–Madrid, 1871)

LA CONSOLACIÓN O MEMORIA DE LA PATRIA

  No siempre, revolviendo
rugiente espuma, azotan
los roncos vendavales
de Albión las canas rocas.
  Ni del Támesis frío
en la opulenta costa
se ven siempre tendidas
las hiperbóreas sombras.
  He aquí ya del Favonio
el aura blanda sopla,
y del pintado Mayo
la cándida luz torna.
  ¿Y será que nosotros
siempre en tenaz congoja
acusemos los hados
que en nuestro mal se gozan?
  ¿A qué llorar en vano
de la española gloria
el fracaso, y los frutos
de la civil discordia,
  y los tristes sucesos
de la suerte azarosa
que de la dulce patria
el caro bien nos roban?
  ¡Oh! demos tregua al pecho,
y afuera las zozobras;
venga el laúd teyano
presto, muchachos, ¡hola!
  Esparce tú aquí en esta
pradera frescas rosas,
y traiga el otro luego
las regaladas copas.
  Que aquí beber yo gusto
a la escondida sombra

DOMINGO MARÍA RUIZ DE LA VEGA

SOLACE OR MEMORY OF THE HOMELAND

  Not ceaselessly the winter gales
with roaring whirling foam
lash the ancient rocks
of Albion.
  Not ceaselessly the hyperborean shades
of frigid Thames
lie swart upon
the opulent shore.
  Now Favonius
exhales its gentle air
and now revives
bright-painted May.
  And shall we still
to sorrow vowed
denounce the fates
that in our sadness joy?
  Why vainly mourn the fallen
glory of Spain
and the fruits
of rebellion,
   and the harsh blows
of fickle destiny
that steal from us the glory
of our dear homeland?
  Oh peace be in our hearts,
our storms be lulled;
bring out the lute boys
and play to us!
  Deck you these meadows
with new rose-buds,
and let him bring us then
rich draughts of wine.
  For it's my pleasure to drink deep
here in the secluded shade

de los gigantes olmos
que a Kensington decoran.
   Del néctar, pues, que envían
de nuestras ricas lomas
los béticos viñedos
henchid las tazas hondas.
   Henchidlas, y de yedra
con vividoras hojas
ornadlas, y bebamos
de la patria en memoria.

of the gigantic elms
of beauteous Kensington.
  Fill then the beakers to the brim
with nectar from
the copious vineyards
of Andalusian hills.
  Oh fill them, and with everlasting
ivy-leaves entwine them,
and we shall toast the homeland
in our memory.

JOSÉ DE ESPRONCEDA
(Almendralejo, Badajoz, 1808–Madrid, 1842)

LA ENTRADA DEL INVIERNO EN LONDRES

> *Un ángulo me basta entre mis lares,*
> *un libro y un amigo, un sueño breve*
> *que no perturben deudas ni pesares.*
> Rioja

Reina tu lobreguez, invierno rudo,
y del norte en los climas ateridos
de sombras y terror tiendes el velo.
Yace sin flores, lánguido, desnudo,
el triste extenso campo y, recogidos
los fulgores del sol, se enluta el cielo.

En el lejano monte
el ronco trueno retumbar se siente,
vuela en el horizonte
el rápido relámpago luciente,
y después en tristura
húndese y en silencio la Natura.

Oye el pastor tranquilo en su cabaña
a la margen sentado de su hoguera
despeñarse las aguas a torrentes;
oye el viento rugir con brava saña
y al lado de su dulce compañera
mira jugar sus niños inocentes;
en su hogar regalado
hasta volver de nuevo a su faena
el labrador cansado
libre de odio, de esperanza y pena,
en la noche horrorosa
se estrecha al seno de su casta esposa.

Medita el sabio en sosegada calma,
en su triste pacífico retiro,
del mísero mortal la infausta suerte.

JOSÉ DE ESPRONCEDA

THE ARRIVAL OF WINTER IN LONDON

> *A corner of my homestead fits me,*
> *a book, a friend, the briefest dream*
> *undisturbed by debts or sorrow.*
>   Rioja

Rude winter, reigns your gloom
and from the North in frozen clime
you draw down the veil of horror and of doom.
Languid and naked, bare of bloom,
stretch the sad fields, and, all withdrawn
their glittering sun, the heavens mourn.

On mountains far-retired
are raucous rolls of thunder heard
and rapid brilliant lightning
darts on the horizon,
till Nature drowns
in silence and in tears.

The peaceful shepherd in his cot
hears, seated by his fireside,
the mighty storm release
torrential rain and roaring gale
and, next his sweet companion, sees
his innocent children play;
delighting in his house
before the morrow's toil
the weary labourer, free
of hatred, hope and pain,
in horrid night lies down to rest
in the chaste bosom of his spouse.

The sage, serene and calm,
studies in peaceful solitude
the luckless fate of mortal man.

Y, embebido en pensar firme su alma,
ni exhala del dolor triste suspiro
ni teme los furores de la muerte.
Tal vez, hórrido invierno,
vuelan tus largas horas venturosas
para el amante tierno
que entre las dichas del placer ansiosas
la boca delicada
avaro besa de su dulce amada.

Salvo de tu furor el marinero
de su Patria feliz arriba al puerto
y saluda la tierra que le encanta;
la tempestad recuerda placentero
que de triste pavor le tuvo yerto
y dulces himnos venturoso canta.
Todos ven sus hogares,
dicha, tranquilidad, gozo y fortuna
reina en sus quietos lares.
Y entre los hielos, al rayar la luna,
ve callada la choza,
callado el muro donde el rico goza.

Mas, ¡ay!, yo, triste, de contino lloro
y de contino crece mi quebranto
y tu horror, ¡estación!, me enluta el alma.
Cuatro veces aquí te vi el tesoro
a los campos robar, tender tu espanto
y derramar terror, silencio y calma.
Palpita el ronco estruendo
de la alterada mar el pecho mío,
el ponto inmenso viendo
que me encadena entre el Bretón sombrío,
y cuyas turbias olas
me alejan de las costas españolas.

Dichoso aquel que del hogar paterno
nunca el umbral dejó, do cariñosa
la apacible virtud meció su cuna;
que recostado en el regazo tierno

His steadfast soul, absorbed in thought,
nor heaves sad sighs of pain
nor fears the pangs of death.
Perhaps, foul winter,
your happy hours fly past
for the warm lover
who, rapt in pleasure,
greedily kisses the soft mouth
of his own dear-beloved.

Safe from your rage, the mariner
joyful comes to port in his Homeland
and kisses the soil of his delighting;
carefree now he calls to mind the storm
which froze him in sad fear
and sings sweet anthems merrily.
All espy their homes,
bliss and peace, joy and good fortune
reign in their quiet homesteads,
they see the quiet cot, the silent walls
of the rich man's castle.

But I, alas, weep endlessly
and endlessly my sad affliction grows
and you, grim season, deck my soul in black.
Four times I've seen you rob the fields of gold,
disseminate your dread,
shed horror, silence, calm.
The raucous din of the rough seas
batters my heart as I look on
the mighty water that imprisons me
in gloomy Britain,
whose wild and turbid waves
estrange me from the coasts of Spain.

Happy the man who never has forsaken
his father's threshold, where peace and virtue
tenderly rocked his cradle;
who, lying in his sweet maid's lap,

de su amada zagala candorosa
le vio dormirse la callada luna.
¡Mil veces venturoso!
Nunca otras tierras vio, nunca agitado
del cuidado enojoso
el sonoro clarín oyó aterrado,
y en su paterno asilo
sus hijos mira en su vejez tranquilo.

Así árbol tierno en el abril florido
libre de la segur, sus tiernas ramas
ostenta al margen del arroyo undoso.
Ya su follaje plácido extendido
libra al ganado de las febeas llamas,
y el canto escucha del pastor quejoso.
En la noche serena
presta acogida al venturoso amante;
brilla la aurora apenas
y levanta su frente rozagante.
Y a su vejez consuelo
dan otros mil reverdeciendo el suelo.

¡Ay!, yo en el suelo de la Patria mía
gocé también la paz; de mi cabaña
orné los juncos de galanas flores;
del Manzanares en la selva umbría
coronado de yedras y espadaña
en mi lira entoné cantos de amores.
En la estación vernosa,
con cuentos mil al lado de la hoguera,
la noche perezosa
pasaba entre las pláticas ligera;
y la naciente aurora
era de nuevas dichas precursora.

Allí gocé del plácido contento
de un tierno corazón amable prenda,
y del primer amor sentí la llama.
Ya fogoso voló mi pensamiento

so innocent and so beloved,
saw the still moon close its eyes in sleep.
Happy a thousand times!
Who never set his eyes on other lands,
who never, in the toils of care,
in terror heard the bugle sound,
and in his ancestral home
gazes on his children, in serene old age.

As the young tree in florid April,
safe from the axe, displays his boughs
along the winding stream.
Now in new leaf, his placid foliage
protects the herd from Phoebus flame
and hearkens to the shepherd's love lament.
In the calm night
he welcomes the happy lover;
at crack of dawn
he raises his luxuriant brow
and hundreds more with their green shade
comfort his age.

Ah! I too on my country's soil
knew peace; I dressed
the reed-thatch of my cot with flowers gay;
In the bosky shade of the Manzanares,
crowned with ivy and bulrush,
I played love songs on my lyre.
In the vernal season
the lazy night passed easily
amid a thousand tales around the fire
in gentle conversation;
and the dawn gold
new joys foretold.

There I enjoyed the sweet content
of a tender loving heart
and of first love I felt the flame.
Already flew my ardent thought

de la alta gloria a la sublime senda
y de mi Patria celebré la fama.
Ora el cañón sonante
que en las cavernas hondas retumbaba,
ora el grito tonante
de Libertad que entre el fragor volaba
mi espíritu movía,
y guerra dije a la maldad impía.

Mas ¿a qué corazón noble y honroso
no engañará la aleve hipocresía
y la traición y ardid tan solapado?
Traición, traición, retumba estrepitoso
Pirene altivo entre su cumbre fría,
del horrísono acento amedrentado.
Traición, traición resuena
hasta el cántabro mar que, removiendo
su recóndita arena
y las costas que baña estremeciendo,
repite el alarido
que entre sus ondas vaga allá perdido.

Adiós, lares queridos, patria mía,
grata a mi pecho más que la riqueza
al del pomposo altivo cortesano,
dulce mansión de gloria y de alegría,
al presente morada de tristeza.
Adiós. Doquier te buscaré, y en vano.
¡Felice el que expirando
al fiero golpe de enhastada lanza
cayó alegre esperando
que fueses libre, y alcanzar venganza
que aún disfrutó el consuelo
de besar al morir el patrio suelo!

Llorar, llorar mi lamentable suerte
me resta en mi desdicha por consuelo
mi idolatrada Patria recordando.
Ni el placer, ni el dolor, ni la atroz muerte

towards the glorious sublime.
I boasted of my storied nation's fame.
Now the booming cannon
in canyons deep resounding,
now the thunderous cry
of Freedom over tumult rising
exalted high my spirit, and I swore
war on impious wickedness.

But oh what noble, honourable hearts
will not be fooled by vile dissembling
and treachery's sly perfidy?
Treachery, treachery, rebounds the cry
from the cold peaks of lofty Pyrenee
at the foul word dumbstruck with fear.
Treachery, treachery echoes loudly
to the far Cantabrian sea,
perturbs its secret sands,
its shores it shuddering laves
and echoes the alarm
which wanders lost there in its waves.

Farewell dear home, my own country,
more pleasing to my heart than wealth
and pomp to the haughty man at court,
sweet residence of glory and of joy,
where now dwells grief alone.
Farewell. I seek you everywhere in vain.
Happy the man though felled
by mighty lance expiring
who held faith in your freedom
and in vengeance; happy he
who knew the solace of embracing
his home soil, dying.

Weeping, lamenting at my sorry fate
is all that I have left for consolation
remembering my own beloved country.
Nor joy, nor pain, nor horrid death

cambian mi faz en tan amargo duelo,
en mi pecho la Patria dominando.
Recostado en la arena
do se estrella feroz la mar bravía,
clamo en mi triste pena:
«Allí está el suelo de la Patria mía»,
y lloroso suspiro,
rica Albión, si tu opulencia miro.

Bajel dichoso, que a la playa cara
que me miró nacer tornas tu prora,
raudo dejando el Támesis undoso,
siempre dulce la mar, serena y clara,
siempre un aura feliz consoladora,
hagan cierto tu rumbo presuroso;
su costa descubriendo
do eterna el sol su claridad derrama,
tu vela en popa hinchando
el alígero viento que la inflama,
dirás con alegría:
«Un desterrado la salud te envía».

disfigure me so bitterly
as my heartache for my homeland.
Here lying on the shore
where breaks the wild ferocious sea
I grieving cry:
'Oh out there far away
is the soil of homeland', and weeping I sigh,
rich Albion, when I your opulence espy.

Oh happy bark who turn your prow
to the sweet shore where I was born
leaving behind the mighty Thames,
good speed, safe voyage may you know,
ever on a calm, bright sea,
ever propelled by a consoling wind;
sighting that coast
whereon the sun eternal pours his light,
the soft wind in your sails,
a wind of fire,
joyfully you'll say:
'an exile sends you health and happiness'.

JOSÉ ALCALÁ GALIANO
(Madrid, 1843–1919)

LONDRES

Pastel de tres millones de mortales,
Especie de lunar sobre la tierra,
Capital en cuestión de *capitales*,
Es Londres, capital de la Inglaterra.

Río de fango que se torna de oro
Con el que a bordo llevan cien navíos,
Dejando cada cual allí un tesoro
Cual dejan en la mar su agua los ríos.

Cielo sin sol y casas culotadas,
Calles do casi viaja el que transita,
Donde hay que hacer lo menos tres jornadas
Para hacer al vecino una visita.

Plazas, palacios, parques y jardines,
Edificios magníficos, museos,
Miladis que parecen serafines,
Niños bonitos y milores feos.

Ricos ante los cuales pordioseros
Parecen nuestros ricos ordinarios;
Pobres ante los cuales caballeros
Nuestros pobres parecen, millonarios.

Eso y mil cosas más muestra la villa
Más grande y populosa de este globo,
Donde, si no hay ladrones en cuadrilla,
Suele haber mercaderes para el robo.

Cerebro de la Europa comerciante,
Capital de la industria, la riqueza,
La libertad, el *Times*, el negociante,
Del *spleen*, de la Biblia y la cerveza.

JOSÉ ALCALÁ GALIANO

LONDON

Muddle of three million mortals,
A kind of blot on the earth,
Capital of Kapital
Is London, England's capital.

Muddy river turning to gold
With cargo of a hundred ships,
Each unloading a new treasure
As rivers feed the sea.

Sunless sky and blackened houses,
Streets where to walk is to embark
On an epic journey, three days travel
To call upon a neighbour.

Squares and palaces, parks and gardens,
Magnificent buildings, museums,
Great ladies with the face of angels,
Pretty children, ugly lords.

Rich men who make our own rich men
Seem beggars; and the poor
Who make our own poor seem
Gentlemen or millionaires.

All this, a thousand other sights, displays
The greatest and most peopled town on earth,
Where, if you're not robbed by gangs of thieves,
There are plenty of merchants to rob you.

Brain of trading Europe,
Capital of industry and wealth,
Liberty, *The Times,* the businessman,
Spleen, the Bible, and beer.

Ved alzarse entre el humo, envuelto en brumas,
Pueblo-almacén que el gran Támesis baña,
Una enorme ciudad que al globo abruma,
Londres, cabeza de la Gran Bretaña.

See rising through the smoke, fog-mantled,
Warehouse-city, lapped by the Thames,
Metropolis that all the world amazes,
London, at Great Britain's head.

MIGUEL DE UNAMUNO
(Bilbao, 1864–Salamanca, 1936)

[LONDRES CON UN SOL LUNÁTICO...]

> *Al partir de Londres, el 2 de marzo, 1936*
> *A Ramón Pérez de Ayala*

Londres con un sol lunático
—por entre la niebla asoma—
ni es Jerusalén ni Roma
sino cine fantasmático;

ceñido de parques reales,
pintada naturaleza,
no realidad, mas realeza;
praderas artificiales;

nubes sumidas en humo;
sueños sumidos en tedio,
que no queda otro remedio
que consumirse en consumo;

muchedumbres en desierto,
soledad entre millones
de mortales que entre sones
mecánicos van al puerto

del morirse soberano;
y viejas con su perrito,
que es el fetiche de un rito
eugénico y malthusiano.

Me vuelvo a ti, madre España,
clara, pobre y cejijunta,
que allí cuando el sol despunta
puedo renovar mi entraña.

> *Londres, 2 de marzo de 1936*

MIGUEL DE UNAMUNO

[LONDON WITH A LUNAR SUN...]

Upon leaving London, March 2nd, 1936
To Ramón Pérez de Ayala

London with a lunar sun –
peeping through the fog –
is not Jerusalem or Rome
but phantom cinema,

ringed with royal parks,
a lily gilded,
royalty and not reality;
artificial meadows,

clouds submerged in smoke,
dreams submerged in boredom,
no remedy remains
but to consume oneself in consumption.

Multitudes in a wasteland,
solitude among millions
of mortals, who amid the din
of traffic go to the harbour

of death sovereign;
and old ladies with lapdogs,
the fetish of a rite
eugenic, Malthusian.

I return to you, bright, poor
and scowling Mother Spain,
so there at the break of day
I may rebuild my heart.

London, March 2nd, 1936

JOSÉ ANTONIO BALBONTÍN
(Madrid, 1893-1978)

PARECÍA EL GUADALQUIVIR

El Támesis estaba en fiesta:
parecía el Guadalquivir.

El espectáculo era nuevo,
dentro de Londres, para mí.
Salí de paseo temprano;
era una mañana de abril
sin una sola nubecilla,
¡qué raro!, en el cielo de añil.
«Dios estaba azul» por completo,
como diría aquel sutil
poeta andaluz, que muriera
descorazonado al sentir,
en las angustias del destierro,
que Dios se había vuelto gris.

Se oía volar a los duendes
como en un cuento de las Mil
y una Noches, y el viejo Támesis
parecía el Guadalquivir.

Gaviotas blancas como lirios,
que simulaban perseguir
no sé qué peces invisibles,
chillaban un gozo infantil.
Unos capullos amarillos
de madreselvas sin abrir
querían volar hacia el cielo
desde lo alto de un pretil.
Cinco niños madrugadores
llenaban el verde jardín
de la orilla de risas claras
como limones del Genil.
Todo sonreía contento

JOSÉ ANTONIO BALBONTÍN

IT SEEMED THE GUADALQUIVIR

The Thames was in carnival:
it seemed the Guadalquivir.

The spectacle was something new,
in the heart of London, new to me.
I went out walking early;
it was an April morning
without a single cloud –
how strange! – in the indigo sky.
'God was blue' utterly so,
as the subtle Andalusian
poet might say, who died
despondent, feeling,
in the anguish of exile,
God had become grey.

You could hear the flying genies
as in a tale from the Thousand
and One Nights, and Old Father Thames
seemed the Guadalquivir.

Lily-white gulls
swooping down to fish for
invisible fish
mewed with a childish delight.
Yellow honeysuckle buds
yet to open
yearned to take flight
from a high parapet.
Five boys, up early,
filled the green garden
on the river bank with laughter
as bright as Genil lemons.
Everything smiled in gladness

de florecer y de vivir
bajo el alba, y el hosco Támesis
parecía el Guadalquivir.

Apareció una barca negra
cual bruja de Shakespeare. La vi
solo unos instantes, pues pronto
se arrebujó en humo, y perdí
la visión de mi paraíso,
como Adán la de su pensil.
Pero yo no había robado
ninguna manzana, y sentí
que me trataba mal la vida.
Callé, no obstante, cual gentil
alumno de Eton, donde nadie
trasluce nunca su sentir.

Volvieron a poco las luces.
No había nadie en el pretil,
ni en el cauce del río oscuro,
ni en el cielo, ni en el jardín,
como si todo hubiera sido
el sueño de una noche de abril.

Y me quedé solo y nostálgico,
soñando en el Guadalquivir.

to flourish and to live
beneath the dawn, and sullen Thames
seemed the Guadalquivir.

A black ship loomed
like a witch from Shakespeare, I saw it
for seconds only, since immediately
it was swallowed up in smoke, I lost
my paradisal vision,
as Adam lost his Eden.
But I had stolen
no apple, and I felt
life was against me,
but I bit my lip,
like an Old Etonian
who never betrays his feelings.

Gradually the light returned.
There was no-one on the parapet,
or in the dark riverbed,
or in the sky, or in the garden,
as if it had all been
an April night's dream.

And I was alone and homesick,
dreaming of the Guadalquivir.

LUIS CERNUDA
(Seville, 1902–Mexico City, 1963)

IMPRESIÓN DE DESTIERRO

Fue la pasada primavera,
Hace ahora casi un año,
En un salón del viejo Temple, en Londres,
Con viejos muebles. Las ventanas daban,
Tras edificios viejos, a lo lejos,
Entre la hierba el gris relámpago del río.
Todo era gris y estaba fatigado
Igual que el iris de una perla enferma.

Eran señores viejos, viejas damas,
En los sombreros plumas polvorientas;
Un susurro de voces allá por los rincones,
Junto a mesas con tulipanes amarillos,
Retratos de familia y teteras vacías.
La sombra que caía
Con un olor a gato,
Despertaba ruidos en cocinas.

Un hombre silencioso estaba
Cerca de mí. Veía
La sombra de su largo perfil algunas veces
Asomarse abstraído al borde de la taza,
Con la misma fatiga
Del muerto que volviera
Desde la tumba a una fiesta mundana.

En los labios de alguno,
Allá por los rincones
Donde los viejos juntos susurraban,
Densa como una lágrima cayendo,
Brotó de pronto una palabra: España.
Un cansancio sin nombre
Rodaba en mi cabeza.
Encendieron las luces. Nos marchamos.

LUIS CERNUDA

PORTRAIT OF EXILE

It was last spring,
Almost a year ago now,
In a drawing-room in the old Inns of Court, London,
Furnished with old pieces. Beyond old buildings
And lawns, the windows gave a distant view
Of the grey lightning of the river.
Everything was grey and seemed exhausted
Like the iris of a sickly pearl.

They were old gentlemen, old ladies,
Dusty feathers in their hats;
A murmur of voices in the corners of the room,
Round tables with vases of yellow tulips,
Family photographs, empty tea-pots.
A shadow falling
Through cat odour
Brought a clatter from the kitchens.

A silent man was sitting
Not far from me. Now and then
I saw the shadow of his long profile
Absently touch the rim of his cup
With the languor of a man
Returned from his tomb
To attend a society tea-party.

On the lips of someone
In the corners of the room
Where the old people murmured together,
Dense as a falling tear,
Blossomed all at once a word: Spain.
A nameless weariness
Rolled round my head.
The lamps were lit. We went away.

Tras largas escaleras casi a oscuras
Me hallé luego en la calle,
Y mi lado, al volverme,
Vi otra vez a aquel hombre silencioso,
Que habló indistinto algo
Con acento extranjero,
Un acento de niño en voz envejecida.

Andando me seguía
Como si fuera solo bajo un peso invisible,
Arrastrando la losa de su tumba;
Mas luego se detuvo.
«¿España?», dijo. «Un nombre.
España ha muerto». Había
Una súbita esquina en la calleja.
Le vi borrarse entre la sombra húmeda.

I went down many stairs in near darkness
And found myself at last in the street,
And saw beside me when I turned
The silent man once again
Who muttered something
In a foreign accent,
Something childish in an old man's voice.

He walked along behind me
Like someone who must bear alone an invisible weight,
Dragging his tombstone with him;
But then he halted.
'Spain?' he said. 'A name.
Spain is dead'. The
Alley veered suddenly.
I saw him vanish in the mist and shadow.

LUIS GABRIEL PORTILLO
(Gimialcón, Ávila, 1907–Watford, 1993)

MI ESPAÑOLA EN LONDRES

   Siempre me espera aunque jamás suspira.
Yo la frecuento cuanto me es posible.
Yacente, no se yergue ni aun me mira.
Mas me ofrenda hermosura inmarcesible.

   Tornada —pudorosa si ostensible—
y absorta en la beldad de su mentira,
su grácil rostro —en el cristal sensible
que Cupido le ofrece— a sí revira.

   Que, ajena a todos, a sí misma se ama.
De rosa, nardo y crema se recama,
y se enflora de fresa en el recuerdo.

   Es ella, en Londres, mi española dama,
y susurro al deciros que hoy se llama
la Venus de Velázquez y el Espejo…

LUIS GABRIEL PORTILLO

IN LONDON, MY LADY OF SPAIN

    Always she waits for me though never she sighs.
I go and see her whenever I am able.
She doesn't even look at me, or rise
from her divan, her beauty imperishable.

    She turns away, chaste but ostensible,
and, brooding on her lovely lies,
she dotes on herself in the susceptible
mirror that Cupid supplies.

    In love with herself, she never has seen us.
Rose-blush and cream burns bright her flame.
In memory blossoms her strawberry stain.

    She is, here in London, my lady of Spain.
Allow me to whisper her anglicized name:
Velázquez's Rokeby Venus…

BASILIO FERNÁNDEZ
(Valverdín, León, 1909–Gijón, Asturias, 1987)

WHY NOT TONIGHT

Aquí, al lado de este fuego fatuo que nos guía,
precedidos de tanta ausente sombra,
seguidos por las nubes,
acabaremos por encontrar nuestra máscara
perdida en el aire matinal, destruida.

¿Por qué, por qué deseo ahora
una atmósfera impregnada de dinamita,
un terremoto tierno dentro de mí
que derrumbe las flores que me desbordan,
las inútiles quejas, toda esta pesadumbre?

Pero la vida sigue su curso sin remedio,
como una piedra echada a rodar al fondo del valle,
como un río que no muere en el mar,
sino que continúa a través de todo
igual que un recuerdo.

A través de todo,
a través de profundas minas y bancos de coral,
de campos de amapolas y atardeceres de verano,
del silencio de esa madre que estrangula a su hijo
y del júbilo de ese general que ahora gana una batalla.

¿Adónde corren los buses sin objeto,
si Jericó pudo caer una tarde como esta,
en que las trompetas y los cláxones sonaban como hoy,
y de un momento a otro puede venirse abajo este artificio
como una torre o un puente,
como esa dama que ahora entra en su Rolls
y está tan cerca de la muerte?

Lo que nos rodea,
lo que nos es lejano,

BASILIO FERNÁNDEZ

WHY NOT TONIGHT

Here, by the will o' the wisp that leads us on,
with so much absent shade before us,
and cloud pursuing us,
we'll find our semblance finally
lost in the morning air, destroyed.

Why, why do I desire now
an atmosphere heavy with dynamite,
a tender earthquake in my entrails
to fell the flowers surfeiting me,
the vain lament, and grieving?

But inexorably life follows its course,
like a stone rolling to the valley bottom,
like a river that doesn't die in the sea,
but goes on flowing through everything
like a memory.

Through everything,
through deep mines and coral reefs,
and poppy fields and summer dusk,
through that mother's silence as she throttles her child,
and through that general's delight at a battle newly won.

Where do the buses rush to aimlessly,
when Jericho fell on an afternoon like this,
when trumpets and horns rang out like out as today,
and all this artifice could come to dust from one moment to the next
like a tower or a bridge,
like that lady now climbing into her Rolls,
who is so close to death.

What surrounds us,
what is far from us,

lo que volverá a suceder,
todo está aquí presente como frutos que se logran en un instante
que descienden a nuestras bocas, y se pudren.

Es cierto, el mundo está habitado de cobardes,
de hombres sin fe que merodean aquí y allí,
que se sumergen y vuelan a la zaga de lo creado...

¿Por qué, por qué esta noche?
Esta noche en que naufrago de Piccadilly a Oxford St.
¿por qué no explota el universo
y me alcanzan sus esquirlas?

¿Para qué esta ilusión si todo se desvanece?
¿Quién puede resistir tanta monotonía
si el caballero que ahora entra en Cannes
es el Guido de Martini
evadido de Siena un día nuboso del 400?

Ante tantos siglos perdidos
esto no tiene objeto.
Las civilizaciones son espumas
sobre el silencio que nos acecha,
y algo de algarabía.

what will happen again,
is present here and now like fruit plucked in a moment
that falls into our mouths and rots.

Truly the world is inhabited by cowards,
faithless men who wander here and there,
who go under, and who whirl in creation's wake…

Why, why tonight?
Tonight when I shipwreck from Piccadilly to Oxford St.
why doesn't the universe explode
and pierce me with its shards?

Why such excitement if everything vanishes?
Who can stand so much monotony
if the gentleman now entering Cannes
is the Guido by Martini
who fled from Siena one cloudy day in 400?

In the face of so many wasted centuries,
this is futile.
Civilisations are froth
on the silence haunting us,
are a mere distraction.

PEDRO BASTERRA [JOSÉ GARCÍA PRADAS]
(Quincoces de Yuso, Burgos, 1910–London, 1988)

LA CORONA DE ELIZABETH II (fragmento)

(…)

La mañana feliz del dos de junio,
conmovida de pechos a banderas,
del Palacio de Buckingham saldrá
la voz clara de heráldicas trompetas;
y al vibrar su pregón de fausto y gloria,
su conjuro, su limpia magia argéntea,
tenderá ante los ojos de las gentes
el antiguo tapiz de la realeza:

Rataplán de tambores masculinos:
alegre el toque, pero el son, de guerra.
Rataplán de gigantes granaderos,
picachos rojos de alta cumbre negra.
Rataplán de dragones a caballo:
danzarina en el aire la cimera;
la luz, guiños del casco a la coraza,
y el porte, reto de la espada enhiesta.

Tras los más arrogantes escuadrones,
tras la marcha triunfal de sol y niebla,
de oro y lauros, de bronces y de cajas,
que suena aún como en las verdes selvas
las áureas trompas de los viejos héroes,
pasan ya los heraldos de librea,
blasonado el tabardo carmesí,
cada cual con las armas de Inglaterra
pendiendo, en paz, del añafil de plata
que hace de ellos figuras arcangélicas;
y detrás, entre *yeomen* y lacayos,
entre gritos de júbilo, que alegran
el revuelo augural de las palomas,
la dorada carroza de la Reina,

PEDRO BASTERRA [JOSÉ GARCÍA PRADAS]

THE CORONATION OF ELIZABETH II (*fragment*)

(…)

On the happy morning of the second of June,
flags and bosoms swollen with pride,
the bright heraldic trumpets will blare out
from Buckingham Palace;
and when their proclamation of fame and glory resounds,
their spell, their silvery magic,
the ancient tapestry of royalty
will lie before the eyes of the peoples.

Tattoo of masculine drums:
joyfully beaten, but warlike in effect.
Tattoo of giant grenadiers,
red peaks with high black tops.
Tattoo of mounted dragoons,
with crests dancing in the wind;
light flashing from helmet to breastplate,
 and their pose, the threat of the upheld sword.

After the more arrogant squadrons,
after the triumphant march of sun and fog,
of gold and laurels, of brass and drums,
still sounding out like the golden horns
of the heroes of old in the greenwood,
now the heralds in livery go past,
with their scarlet tabards emblazoned,
each one with the arms of England
hanging, at rest, from the silver bugles
which make them look like archangels;
and behind, surrounded by yeomen and lackeys,
and cries of joy that arouse
the prophetic swooping of pigeons,
the Queen's Gold State Coach,

mitológica en tallas y pinturas,
coronada, aire-altiva de cimeras,
con sus ocho pedreses windsoreños
de humillado frontal, que, por parejas,
regirán cuatro regios postillones
de chupilla escarlata y gorra negra.

   Rodará la carroza por el Mall
hacia el arco triunfal que al fin la espera
y, al pasar, el famoso Almirantazgo,
tremolante de grímpolas la antena,
tendrá el aire de un barco de batalla
que al puerto vuelve con victoria y presas.

   Caerá sobre ella, cuando pase el arco
y augusta ruede por Trafalgar Square,
la aquilina mirada del gran Nelson,
y a su mismo interior irá la seña
que el Estuardo infeliz hace a los reyes
cuando van a encontrar al pueblo en Westminster.

   Rodará por Whitehall, solar de príncipes;
pasará el Cenotafio de dos guerras,
que lo que hay que pagar por libertades
a los pueblos británicos recuerda;
y, al entrar en la plaza de los fastos
decisivos, primer lar de Inglaterra,
desde el puente de Westminster un ¡hurra!
lanzará en su cuadriga Boadicea,
si el intrépido Cromwell, más abajo
—con sus leyes de espada y Biblia a medias,
puritano y marcial su regio orgullo,
falso aún su desdén de la realeza—,
verá impávido, al pie del Parlamento,
la prez bizarra de las guardias regias...

   Llegará el real cortejo a la Abadía,
que ocupa el sitio que ocupó la iglesia
de Eduardo Primero el Confesor
y siete siglos de horas magnas cuenta.

mythological in its carvings and decorations,
crowned, in proud crests,
with its eight Windsor Greys,
heads lowered, guided in pairs
by four Yeomen of the Guard
in scarlet coats and black caps.

   The coach will descend the Mall
to the triumphal arch at the bottom,
and, as it goes through, the famous Admiralty,
its mast aflutter with flags,
will seem a battleship
returned to port victorious with captives.

   Beyond the Arch, wheeling proudly
through Trafalgar Square, the aquiline
gaze of great Nelson will fall on it,
and into will come the wave
the unlucky Stuart sends to the royals
on their way to Westminster and the people.

   It will roll on down Whitehall, home to princes;
it will pass the Cenotaph, memorial of two wars,
reminder to the British peoples
of the price of freedom;
and, as it enters the square of the final
pageantry, the first house of England,
Boudicca will shout a hurrah!
from her chariot on Westminster Bridge,
even if bold Cromwell, further down –
brandishing his sword and his Bible,
his puritan warlike royal pride,
still with his false disdain for kings –
will look on unmoved at the splendour
of the royal guard by the Houses of Parliament…

   The royal procession will arrive at the Abbey,
which stands where stood the church
of Edward I, the Confessor,
and is a magnificent seven centuries old.

Ya esperada en el atrio de Poniente
por el clero mitrado —y, en cabeza,
por los dos principales arzobispos,
de Cantórbery y York—, la joven Reina
llegará al sacro templo; se alzará
de un davídico salmo, al entrar ella,
la solemne oración, y así que ponga
pie en la nave central, las voces frescas
de la Westminster School, voces de infantes
que exultarán de gozo al conocerla,
se alzarán jubilosas aclamándola
con su *Vivat Regina Elizabetha!*...

   Y habrá un pasmo de pompa sangri-azul,
de oficial bizarría, de grandeza
titular y de arreos peregrinos
en el gótico marco de la escena
—recargado de regios personajes,
pares, lores del Reino y de la Iglesia,
damas, *knights*, dignatarios del país,
Commonwealth y naciones extranjeras—
cuando avance hacia el Sur, por el estrado
que entre coro y altar se alzó, la Reina.

(...)

Awaited at the Western entrance
by mitred clergy, with the two archbishops,
of York and of Canterbury,
at their head, the young Queen
will arrive at the holy temple; as she enters,
a solemn prayer, a psalm of David
will be prayed, and, as soon as she sets foot
in the nave, the fresh voices
of the Westminster School choir, voices of children
who will be filled with delight when they meet her,
will be raised, joyfully acclaiming her
with their *Vivat Regina Elizabetha!*…

   And there will be the wondrous sight of blue-blood pomp,
of civil splendour, of titled gentry,
of exotic trappings
amid the Gothic architecture –
ornamented with royal personages,
peers, lords of the land and of the church,
ladies, knights, dignitaries from the home nation,
the Commonwealth and abroad –
when she advances southwards over the platform
erected between choir and altar: the Queen.

(…)

JOSÉ MARÍA AGUIRRE RUIZ
(1924-¿?)

EL TÁMESIS

En esta fábrica de brumas
Y de verdes dragones corrosivos,
Que devoran el sol perpetuamente,
Ya no sois portadores
Del agua de la multiplicación.
Todo lo habéis trocado
Por correas sin fin,
Sobre las cuales fluyen
Cuervos negros y asesinas espumas
Y residuos de águilas,
En otro tiempo blancas y volando
Sobre el espejo bruñido del amor.
¿Qué habéis hecho de tanta belleza como fluía
Bajo el suavísimo seudónimo de Támesis?
¡Que tengamos que soportar tanta corrosión
Por esta avidez vuestra por convertir
Metálicos planetas
En astro abrasador de nuestras sombras!
La lepra solo nos han dejado en la mirada
De este febril alambique de desperdicios.

JOSÉ MARÍA AGUIRRE RUIZ

THE THAMES

On this factory of fog
And green corrosive dragons,
Constantly devouring the sun,
You no longer now are bearers
Of the waters of multiplication.
You have exchanged it all
For endless conveyor-belts,
Over which flow
Black crows and murderous foam
And residues of eagles,
Once white and flying over
The burnished mirror of love.
What have you done with all the beauty that flowed
Under the soft, soft nom de plume of Thames?
Oh that we must bear so much corrosion
Because of the greed with which you convert
Metallic planets
Into this star which consumes our shadows!
All they have left us to gaze on is the leprosy
Of this febrile distillation of waste.

MANUEL PADORNO
(Santa Cruz de Tenerife, 1933–Madrid, 2002)

CHARING CROSS

FRAGMENTO PRIMERO

22.9.71

En un lugar, río Támesis, Charing Cross
desde el que pueden verse grandes lienzos lisos de lona rugosos
 colgados,
altos edificios planos, paneles entre la gasa y el gas de la
 niebla engañosa,
botes de cerveza, ventanas encendidas por dentro

este largo muro se desliza ante mí, corre la pétrea piedra tallada
 por la maestra mano inmóvil,
la larga construcción fluye veloz en la poesía del siglo XX

Estar aquí (o vivir todavía) tiene sus inconvenientes cuando
es lugar codiciado, de pronto, el golpe de vista hacia lo más
 oscuro, en momentos de terrible tensión, mear

huele la flor de orín, desflecada flor contra la pulida talla
 de piedra,
piel de serpiente, muelle, donde apoyar los brazos y posar la mirada y
 atinar, qué terrible, en un punto donde se trabe y trabaje

mirar largamente cómo pasa el río de John Donne, el agua a motor
 llena de asientos que flotan
con turistas de todas las nacionalidades

el barco gris inmóvil deja una estela bulliciosa sobre su propia
 cama plana movediza

Arrojar entonces desde el puente la mirada que repta y tacta y
 palpa. El tacto del ojo humano
Cómo detrás de un lienzo gris cercano con algunas figuras reclinadas

MANUEL PADORNO

CHARING CROSS

FIRST FRAGMENT

22.9.71

In a place, river Thames, Charing Cross
from where may be seen great plain wrinkled canvases
   hanging,
high flat buildings, panels in the gauze and gas
   of the deceptive mist,
beer-cans, lit windows

this long wall slides by me, the massy stone carved by the motionless
   master's hand rushes past,
the long construction flows rapidly into 20th century poetry

Being here (or staying alive) has its drawbacks when
it's the desired place, suddenly to glimpse the deepest
   dark, in moments of terrible tension, the leaf-rusted

flower smells of pee, frayed flower against the polished
   stone,
snake-skin, wharf, where one may rest one's arms and look
   and see, how awful, in a place where one is doing one's utmost

to contemplate John Donne's river flowing, water with motorboats
   full of seats afloat
with tourists from every nation

the motionless grey boat leaves a boisterous wake on its own
   flat shifting bed

To cast then from the bridge the crawling tactile squeezing
   gaze. The touch of the human eye
As behind a grey nearby canvas with reclining figures

desciende otro gris borroso y más allá una tela mayor *orange* violeta
  se difumina, cae
rompe el contorno, es decir, saltan las grapas y se derraman, lejos
  Rothko

sucede enfrente, por la izquierda y hacia atrás
Bulle el parque con sus ventanas vegetales iluminadas, gaseosos
  árboles fosforescentes,
cortinas que desprenden una luz cúbica cerrada en cada piso

El alto oleaje de la orquesta de los Royal Horse Guards avanza
  sobre los espectadores, en batería
aplasta las señoras cremas que vi al bajar, acribilla a los
  más lejanos transeúntes

Grises paneles forman parte de la enorme sala de la ciudad
  acordada al río,
alguien podría reconstruirlos con solo vaciar gran cantidad
  de cubos de literatura,
y toda esta zona es propia para la fotografía y el industrioso
  fotograma
(aquí, roto el poema lógico, recurre él mismo a la voz de la
  calle Inverness Terrace, consciente de que
ese coche que pasa por su imaginación, no para concluir o
  cerrar este viejo trabajo milenario
sino para empezarlo en realidad en el mismo silencio que queda
  aquí debajo, en blanco, en esta página hospitalaria)
  recordándote

Fue entonces cuando le di a entender que aquella canción estaba escrita
  en el siglo XIII
y respondía a normas tradicionales, es decir, que aquel paraje
no había sido hollado antes, usado nunca, su ritmo el habla
  escrita

10.10.71

  Sin vigilar este proceso lógico
y tal vez con deseos de iniciar su consumación, de concluir
  sus principios

there falls another blurry grey and beyond a larger orange
   violet curtain fades, descends
breaks the frame, or, say, the staples fail and it spills, far off
   Rothko

happens over there, on the left and behind me
The park seethes with its vegetal lit windows, gaseous
   phosphorescent trees,
curtains emitting a closed cubic light on every floor

The high tide of the Royal Horse Guards band advances
   on the crowd, in a battery
it crushes the cream ladies I saw when I came out, it riddles the
   furthest-away passers-by

Grey panels form part of the vast city hall
   parallel to the river,
someone could reconstruct them simply by emptying out numerous
   buckets of literature,
and this whole area is apt for photography and the industrious
   movie-still
(here the logical poem breaks, he himself has recourse to the voice of
   Inverness Terrace, aware that
the car travelling through his imagination, not to conclude or
   close this old millenary work
but in fact to begin it, in the same silence to be found
   here below, white, on this hospital page)
   remembering you

That's when I told him that the music had been written
   in the Thirteenth Century
and followed traditional rules, that is to say, that place
was virgin soil, its rhythm written
   speech

10.10.71

   Paying no attention to this logical process
and perhaps wishing to begin its completion, to conclude
   its beginnings

solo silabeé, la voz yo no sé qué, sin escribir nada ni siquiera
   intentar recordarlo

Por aquel decorado de largas calles *físicas*,
altos muros abiertos y puertas encendidas
brota el mármol de la petrificada fuente,
niños de piedra inmóvil saltan a la plaza *humanos*,
tendidas estatuas femeninas por el suelo de yerba se incorporan
   vestidas de piedra luminosa,
autobuses llenos de maniquíes regresan a sus casas para vestirse
   con su piel, *desnudos*
gente parada como si fuera un río inmóvil, de pie, pintado humo
   en el cielo,
bandadas de palomas picoteadas por las baldosas de Trafalgar
   Square.
Flota la luz y florea: un mundo vegetal inmóvil deslizándose hacia
   la quietud más pétrea, líquida
flora de cristal humano

Yo bajé aquellas calles mecánicamente pensativo, sin pensar
(pienso si la textura del poema se me viene imponiendo)
hasta llegar a las orillas de la piedra fluvial
(aquí, incapaz de describir tal paisaje, o dar memoria de él)
   solo me atengo
(no en persecución o búsqueda de este mismo trabajo. Al contrario,
   prescindiendo de él si fuera necesario, posible, y en
   busca de mi propia persecución)
a reflejar un hecho que
a primera vista pudiera parecer que me concierne pura y
   exclusivamente,
a mi mentalidad personal y, sin embargo, tan espantosa duda hace
que prosiga, aún atacando a fondo el propio juego del poema,
es decir, poner en sumo peligro y de forma temeraria
la consecuencia lógica del canto
(si he relegado lo que en un principio
iba a ser el final del poema Charing Cross a un lugar, en el
   tiempo más tardío,
no en el espacio, pues puede irse a él solo indicando a pie
   de página
y al correr de los ojos allí, o aquí)

I only uttered syllable by syllable, in no particular voice, not writing
    anything down or trying to remember it

Through that decor of long *physical* streets,
high open walls and lit-up doors
sprouts the marble of the petrified fountain,
human children set in stone jump down onto the square,
statues of women lying on the grass sit up
    dressed in luminous stone,
buses full of mannequins return home to put on
    their skin, *naked*
people halted like a motionless river, upright, painted smoke
    in the sky,
flocks of pigeons pecked by the paving-stones of Trafalgar
    Square.
Light floats and flowers: an immobile vegetal world sliding into
    the stoniest stillness, liquid
flora of human crystal

I went down those streets mechanically pensive, unthinking
(I think whether the poem's texture is imposing itself on me)
till I reach the banks of the flowing stone
(here, incapable of describing such a landscape, or memorialising it)
    I restrict myself
(not in pursuit of or researching this same work. On the contrary,
    dispensing with it if it were necessary, possible, and seeing my own
    pursuit)
to considering a fact which
at first might seem to concern me and
    me only,
my own mentality and, yet, such a fearful doubt makes
me go on, still delving deep into the game of the poem,
which is to say, putting in the greatest danger, boldly so,
the logical consequence of the song
(if I have deferred what initially
was going to be the end of the poem Charing Cross to a place, later
    in time,
not in space, since one can get to it just by pointing to the foot
    of the page
and running one's eyes here, or there)

ahora, restituyendo al fin el final del poema, en Madrid, y en
    su lugar predilecto,
       los versos últimos
(siempre que se le dé la forma tradicional). He de convenir

que si bajé las calles ¿fue una estrategia de mi paseo o lo es
    del poema?
(posiblemente me encontrara en Leicester Square)
hasta Charing Cross (desde
donde pude ver) no sin curiosidad y asombro, cómo
los altos edificios iban desmoronándose en lisas lonas colgadas,
blancos paneles en la niebla y exclamé
este es el final: aquí termina.

now putting the end of the poem back to the end, in Madrid, and in
 its favourite place,
 the last lines
(provided tradition is respected). I have to agree

that if I went down the streets – was that part of the plan of my walk or
 of the poem? –
(I might have found myself in Leicester Square)
to Charing Cross (where
I could see from) not without curiosity and amazement, how
the high buildings were collapsing into plain hanging canvases,
white panels in the mist and I exclaimed
this is it: this is the end.

RAFAEL GUILLÉN
(Granada, 1933)

DE LA MATERIA DE LOS TAXIS

De nuevo te esperé en el desconsuelo
de la esquina. Por el bullicio oscuro
iban, venían rojos autobuses,
acharolados taxis que, ocupados,
se detenían un segundo antes
del desencanto. La farola daba
entintado de *comic* a la espera.

Los taxis están hechos con materia
de soledad, de presurosos besos,
de palabras sin terminar, de rápidos
adioses, de cabezas que se vuelven
como pidiendo auxilio. Cada taxi
va tejiendo y tejiendo su capullo
de seda por las calles, va encerrando
su mariposa entre los hilos tensos
de la ciudad que gime y que lo envuelve.

¿Por qué querer es esperar? La lluvia
tenaz parpadeaba en el cambiante
neón de Piccadilly y los neumáticos
por el asfalto húmedo sonaban
como el desuello de una piel inmensa.
Todo el desecho de la prisa iba
acumulado en los asientos turbios
de los taxis. Su tántalo destino
era llegar para volver de nuevo.

Los taxis se alimentan de colillas,
de tersos portafolios, de monturas
de gafas, de coronas funerarias,
de perfumados guantes, de pañuelos
inmundos, de paraguas olvidados.
El horizonte de los taxis nace

RAFAEL GUILLÉN

THE STUFF OF TAXIS

I stood waiting for you again on this dismal
corner. Through the bustling dark
red buses came and went, and shiny black
cabs with people in them stopped a moment
before all hopes were dashed. The streetlamp cast
ink as from a comic on the waiting.

Taxis are made of the stuff of solitude,
of hasty kisses, of words broken-off,
of rapid goodbyes, of heads turning back
as if to call for help. Each taxi weaves
and weaves its silk cocoon through the streets,
enclosing its butterfly in the tense threads
of the city that moans and engulfs it.

Why is to love to wait? The stubborn rain
flickered in the flashing Piccadilly neon,
and taxis on the wet tarmac sounded like
the flaying of an immense skin.
The detritus of speed was heaped
on the taxis' turbulent seats. Their eternal fate
was to reach their destination, and depart again.

Taxis feed on stubbed-out cigarettes,
polished briefcases, spectacle-frames,
funeral wreaths, scented gloves, used
handkerchiefs, and left-behind umbrellas.
The taxis' horizon is born behind the back
of light, is peopled with sanatoria
and surgeries, borders on traffic-lights,
is routed through commerce and panic and dossiers.

Where does love go when it stands us up?
A sluggish stream of raindrops

a espaldas de la luz, está poblado
de sanatorios y consultas, linda
con discos y semáforos, discurre
por negocios y apremios y legajos.

¿A dónde va el amor cuando no acude
a nuestra cita? Una lenta hilera
de gotas resbalaban por el borde
de la farola anochecida. Un golpe
de tos quebrada restalló muy cerca
de mi bufanda. El viento me azuzaba
los mastines del frío. Y otros taxis
pasaban sin parar, como otras noches,
como todas las noches de mi vida.

Cuando al amanecer se quedan solos
los taxis, se acarician la gastada
tapicería, que conserva algunas
viejas huellas de semen o de lágrimas.

Londres, 12 de mayo 1990

slid down the streetlamp gone dark.
A coughing-fit exploded near my scarf.
The wind loosed the dogs of cold onto me.
And, as on other nights, more taxis passed
and didn't stop,
as on every evening of my life.

    At dawn when they're alone,
the taxis stroke their worn
upholstery still spotted with
old tracks of semen or of tears.

London, May 12th, 1990

CARLOS SAHAGÚN
(Onil, Alicante, 1938–Madrid, 2015)

VIVIÓ AQUÍ

De nuevo en Londres, la tristeza o el tedio, la vejez
agazapada en las salas de espera, el merodeo
por lugares insólitos, la noche en los relojes,
y en la luz vacilante la dolorosa rúbrica
de los borrachos y los solitarios,
únicos seres vivos en el silencio invicto.

¿Vivió aquí alguna vez mi juventud?

CARLOS SAHAGÚN

HERE LIVED

Back in London, melancholy or boredom, old age
slumped in waiting-rooms, loitering
in unfamiliar places, night on the clocks,
and in the flickering light the dismal rubric
of drunks and loners,
the only living creatures in the all-conquering silence.

Were my young years lived here once?

JUAN ANTONIO MASOLIVER RÓDENAS
(Barcelona, 1939)

[DESPUÉS DE HABER ESTADO ENTRE LOS MERCADERES...]

Después de haber estado entre los mercaderes
del templo de la sabiduría de Euston
Centre, entre fariseos de grises sotanas
de funcionario y damas ligeramente
amargas, ahítos todos en el ejercicio
de la justicia, protegido tan solo
por la mejor de las tres personas
que comparten la divinidad, salí
a purificarme en el agua
del retrete y a borrar mi fracaso
en la cervecería de la esquina, y luego
regresé a Fordwych Road a buscar
el consuelo que buscan los perros
con collar perdidos en las calles
de la niebla o los niños que perdieron
a su madre en algún lecho ajeno,
en los baldaquines de los arzobispos
o de aquel sacerdote supremo
de Regent Street con las uñas
perpetuamente enjabonadas y
la dolorida mirada de los virtuosos
condenados a orinar en un lavabo público.
Regresé a Fordwych Road por avenidas
de un luminoso otoño, amansado
por el dulce mediodía del amor
y los árboles. Llamé, abriste la puerta
y caí al pozo.

JUAN ANTONIO MASOLIVER RÓDENAS

[AFTER I HAD BEEN AMONG THE TRADERS...]

After I had been among the traders
in the temple of wisdom of Euston
Centre, among pharisees in grey
bureaucratic robes and disenchanted
ladies, all of them surfeited with
the exercise of justice, protected only
by the best of the three persons
in God, I went to purify myself
in water in the lavatory, and to drink
away my failure in the pub on the
corner, then I returned to Fordwych
Road to look for the solace lost
collared dogs seek in foggy streets,
or children who lost their mother
in some stranger's bed,
in the canopies of archbishops
or of that high priest
of Regent Street with his perpetually
soapy fingernails and the dolorous
expression of the virtuous
condemned to urinate in a public toilet.
I returned to Fordwych Road through avenues
of light-filled autumn, lulled
by the sweet midday of love and trees.
I rang the bell, you opened the door
and I fell down the well.

JUAN LUIS PANERO
(Madrid, 1942–Torroella de Montgrí, Gerona, 2013)

LO QUE QUEDA DESPUÉS DE LOS VIOLINES

Cuando te olvides de mi nombre,
cuando mi cuerpo sea solo una sombra
borrándose entre las húmedas paredes de aquel cuarto.
Cuando ya no te llegue el eco de mi voz
ni el resonar cordial de mis palabras,
entonces, te pido que recuerdes que una tarde,
unas horas, fuimos juntos felices y fue hermoso vivir.
Era un domingo en Hampstead, con la frágil primavera
de abril posada sobre los brotes de los castaños.
Pasaban hacia la iglesia apresuradas monjas
irlandesas, niños, endomingados y torpes, de la mano.
Arriba, tras los setos, en la verde penumbra
del parque dos hombres lentamente se besaban.
Tú llegaste, sin que me diera cuenta apareciste y empezamos a hablar
tropezando de risa en las palabras, titubeantes
en el extraño idioma que ni a ti ni a mí pertenecía.
Después te hiciste pequeña entre mis brazos
y la hierba acogió tu oscura cabellera.
A veces las cosas son simples y sencillas
como mirar el mar una tarde en la infancia.
Luego la escalera gris, larga y estrecha,
la alfombra con ceniza y con grasa,
tus pequeños pechos desolados en mi boca.
Sí, a veces es sencillo y es hermoso vivir,
quiero que lo recuerdes, que no olvides
el pasar de aquellas horas, su esperanzado resplandor.
Yo también, lejos de ti, cuando perdida en la memoria
esté la sed de tu sonrisa, me acordaré, igual que ahora,
mientras escribo estas palabras para todos aquellos
que un momento, sin promesas ni dádivas, limpiamente se entregan.
Desconociendo razas o razones se funden
en un único cuerpo más dichoso
y luego, calmado ya el instinto
y rezumante de estrenada ternura el corazón,

JUAN LUIS PANERO

AFTER THE MUSIC, WHAT REMAINS

When you forget my name,
when my body is only a shadow
erasing itself between the damp walls of that room.
When you no longer hear the echo of my voice
nor the warm sound of my words,
then, I beg you to remember that one afternoon,
for a few hours, we were happy together and life was beautiful.
It was a Hampstead Sunday, the fragile April spring
resting on the budding chestnut-trees.
Irish nuns were hurrying to church, holding by the hand
sleepy children in their Sunday best.
Further uphill, in the shrubbery, in the green
penumbra of the park, two men kissed languorously.
You came along, appeared without me noticing, and we began talking,
stumbling over our words in laughter, teetering
in the strange language that was neither yours or mine.
Then you curled up in my arms
and your dark hair on the grass.
Sometimes thing are simple and straightforward
as gazing at the sea on an afternoon in childhood.
Then the grey stairs, long and narrow,
ash and grease-stains on the carpet,
your little nipples desolate in my mouth.
Yes, at times living is easy and lovely,
I want you to remember that, and not forget
the passage of those hours, their hopeful radiance.
I too, far away from you, when the thirst
of your smile is lost in memory, shall remember, as now,
while I write these words for all who, promising nothing,
freely give themselves to one another.
With no thought of race or reason they melt
into one more blissful body
and then, desire assuaged, and the heart
now brimming over with tenderness,

se separan y cumplen su destino,
sabiendo que quizá solo por eso
su existir no fue en vano.

they part and fulfil their destiny,
in the knowledge that, perhaps just because of this,
they did not exist in vain.

PERE GIMFERRER
(Barcelona, 1945)

PUENTE DE LONDRES

> *¿Encontraría a la Maga?*

—Eres tú, amigo? —dije.
—Deséale suerte a mi sombrero de copa.
Una dalia de cristal
trazó una línea verde en mi ojo gris.
El cielo estaba afónico como un búho de níquel.
—Adiós, amigo —dije.
—Echa una hogaza y una yema de huevo en mi bombín.
Una bombilla guiñaba entre las hojas de acanto.
Mi corazón yacía como una rosa en el Támesis.

PERE GIMFERRER

LONDON BRIDGE

Would I meet the Sorceress?

'Is it you, friend?', I said.
'Wish my top-hat good luck'.
A glass dahlia
drew a green line on my grey eye.
The sky was as mute as a nickel owl.
'Goodbye, friend', I said.
'Throw a loaf and an egg-yolk in my hat'.
A light-bulb blinked in the acanthus leaves.
My heart lay like a rose upon the Thames.

GUILLERMO CARNERO
(Valencia, 1947)

RETORNO A GREENWICH PARK

> *More dear, both for themselves*
> *and for thy sake.*
> WORDSWORTH

Don de la soledad, me has alcanzado
tantas veces que al fin has convertido
el accidente de tu desaliento
en más sabia y mejor naturaleza.

Tu enseñanza me asiste en los instantes
que se anegan en luz cuando amanece,
y puedo ver mi rostro en la paz de tu espejo
con mayor nitidez y certidumbre.

El invierno me trae a este jardín
donde las ramas trizan el cristal del poniente,
y su negrura lleva mi mirada
hacia el error que aflige al pensamiento:

orilla los parterres como un lobo aterido
receloso del gris del cieno helado,
y la desolación de sus pupilas
finge esperar un signo de la nieve.

Los senderos remontan la ladera
hasta desvanecerse entre los olmos;
allí, bajo la sombra, se cobijan
lugares escondidos donde estuve.

«No los pienses, me gritan las gaviotas.
Aprende a conocer en otra hondura.
La verdad acontece con el daño.
Escucha la lección de la marea».

GUILLERMO CARNERO

REVISITING GREENWICH PARK

> *More dear, both for themselves*
> *and for thy sake.*
> WORDSWORTH

Gift of solitude, you have kept me company
so many times that you have finally transformed
the accident of your dismay
into a wiser and a better nature.

Your lesson is with me in the moments
flooded with light when the day dawns,
and I can see my face in your peaceable mirror
more clearly, more assuredly.

Winter brings me to these gardens
where branches break the glass of dusk,
and their blackness raises my eyes
towards the error that distresses thought:

it skirts the parterres like a chilled-through wolf
fearful of the frozen mud,
and its desolate pupils
feign a hopeful hint of snow.

The footpaths climb the hill
and vanish in the elms;
there in the shadows shelter
the hidden places once I visited.

'Forget about them', shriek the gulls.
'Learn the deeper knowledge.
Truth comes through pain.
Attend to the teaching of the tide'.

El mar asciende lento en su rumor oscuro
a diluirse en el azul del río,
y la memoria inunda la conciencia
ungiendo la aridez de sus orillas

con el color radiante de los días
en que estallaba el oro del verano,
con su luz cenital, cúpula ardiente
donde volaban alto los sentidos.

Tu risa rebosaba de las fuentes,
tu calor era sangre en el salto del ciervo,
y la elasticidad de tu cintura
se mecía en la calma de los cisnes.

Por tus ojos miraba el amarillo
de la arrogancia de los tulipanes,
la gota azul al borde de la hoja,
el verde esplendoroso de la hierba.

Ahora cae la noche, y en el último tren,
que corta la quietud como una herida,
pongo en palabras míseras los ecos del poema
que escribiste en el agua y en las nubes.

The seas slowly rise with their mysterious noise
to be diluted in the blue of the river,
and memory floods consciousness
anointing the dryness of its banks

with the radiant colour of the days
when golden summer erupted,
its lit zenith, burning dome
where senses flew so high.

Your laughter flowed from the fountains,
your warmth was blood by the deer-leap,
and your supple waist
swayed to the peace of the swans.

With your eyes I saw the vainglorious
yellow of the tulips,
the blue droplet on the leaf,
the green splendour of the grass.

Now night is falling, and in the last train,
cutting through the quiet like a wound,
I put into grieving words the echo of the poem
you wrote on the water, in the clouds.

LEOPOLDO MARÍA PANERO
(Madrid, 1948–Las Palmas de Gran Canaria, 2014)

CONDESA MORFINA

Y llegaron los húngaros bailando,
      y ya era tarde
pero bajo la noche practicaron su arte
y en la noche tú, hermana,
me diste la mano.
      (La gitana predijo y repredijo
pero la noche seguía su curso
y en la noche escuché tu abrazo
correcto y silencioso,
     señora
hermosísima dama
      que en la noche juegas
un blanco juego. (Hermosísima dama
serena y afligida
     violeta nocturna
hermosísima dama
      que la noche protege,
que en la noche vela
noche cándida y helada
      (pura como el hielo
pura como el hielo tú eres, hermosa dama,
Madonna en el viento
      hermosa y dulce dama
que me libras de pobreza
     per amor soi gai
alegría de la nada,
     hermosa dama
hermosa y dulce dama en mi
      pensamiento
Tell me
  I get the Blue for you
dime tus sombras lentamente
despacio como si anduviéramos
como si bajo la noche anduviéramos

LEOPOLDO MARÍA PANERO

COUNTESS MORPHINE

And here came Hungarians dancing,
          and it had got late
but under the night they practised their art
and in the night you, sister,
took me by the hand.
        (The gipsy-woman told fortune after fortune
but the night pursued its course
and in the night I heard your formal
silent embrace,
    my lady
so beautiful
    you who play at night
your white game. (Lady so beautiful
serene, afflicted
      nocturnal violet
my lady so beautiful
         who the night watches over,
who keeps the night watch
the frozen white night
      (pure as ice
pure as ice you are, my lady so beautiful.
Madonna in the wind
        beautiful sweet lady
who raises me from poverty
        per amor soi gai
joy of nothingness,
      beautiful lady
beautiful sweet lady in my
       thoughts
Tell me
  I get the Blue for you
tell me your shadows slowly
slowly as though we were walking
as though we were walking under the night

tú que andas sobre la nieve.
                    Y aterido de frío, por el
                            Puente de Londres
                        —*is going to fall*—
por el puente de Londres, manos en los bolsillos
y el río debajo, triste y sordo
no era un dulce río
mis ojos apenas veían
pero sabía que mi hermana me esperaba
no era un dulce río
sopesando el bien y el mal en una fulgurante balanza
mi triste hermana me esperaba
                        Monelle
me cogió de la mano
poderosa e impotente como un niño
llamándome en la sombra, con voz escasa
con voz escasa y tus harapos blancos, llamándome en la sombra,
hermosísima dama.
              Y con la mano
frágil y descarnada tú apagabas, y con el roce,
con el roce, en la sombra, de tus blancos harapos
tú apagabas las lágrimas
                    deshacías el dolor en pequeñas láminas
harapienta princesa,
              tú me diste la mano.
(Y bajo la noche caminaba, buscándola a ella
por suburbios de Londres, a la niña harapienta
vista en todos los rostros de las prostitutas
un frío invierno de 1850
harapienta princesa.
De entre el sudor, la oscuridad, el miedo,
el temblor sordo de la vida,
su dura confusión, su almacenar sombrío
surgió aquella niña, aquel rostro que busco
aquel recuerdo triste y esta luz que rescata
una tarde de 1850
aquella niña
        y en la habitación vacía
                        (y ya era tarde)

you who walk over snow.
                              And cold to the bone, over
                                    London Bridge –
                                      is falling down –
over the London bridge, hands in pockets
and the river below, sad and muffled
was no sweet river
my eyes could hardly see
but I knew my sister was waiting for me
it was no sweet river
weighing good and evil in dazzling scales
my sad sister was waiting for me
                                      Monelle
took me by the hand
powerful and powerless as a child
calling to me in the shadows, faintly
faintly in your white rags, calling to me in the shadows,
so beautiful lady.
                       And with your fragile
emaciated hand you quelled, and with the rustle,
with the rustle, in the shadows, of your white rags
you quelled my tears
                            you tore my pain to shreds
princess in rags
                    you took me by the hand
(and under the night I walked, searching for her
through London suburbs, for the girl in rags
seen in all the prostitutes' faces
in the cold winter of 1850
ragged princess.
From the sweat, the dark, the fear,
the dull tremor of life,
its harsh muddle, its grim warehouse
emerged that girl, that face I look for,
that sad memory, and this light that brings back
an afternoon in 1850
that girl)
            and in the empty room
                              (and it had got late)

yo cojo el azul
                para ti
aguja que excava la carne que ya no siente
                                      y ya era tarde
pero bajo la noche practicaron su arte.

I get the blue
         for you
needle excavating now numb flesh
                              and it had got late
but under the night they practised their art.

RAFAEL ARGULLOL
(Barcelona, 1949)

12-III-2013

Entre las cinco y las seis de la tarde:
hora punta en Londres.
El ángel tutelador de ciudades
se muestra sorprendido, un día más,
por la precisión del engranaje.
Como marionetas en manos de un comediante invisible,
los pobres seres humanos
corren velozmente de aquí para allá,
expulsados por las transparentes torres de Babel,
arrastrados por demonios entre niebla y asfalto,
empujados por las furias hacia los orificios del subsuelo.
Cada día se ejecuta la misma ceremonia:
el vértigo que devora a criaturas
con prisa y sin destino.
El ángel observa, melancólico,
cómo las calles se vacían con prontitud.
Ha tutelado a los hombres desde la fundación de Uruk.
Ha vigilado el auge y la caída
de Nínive, de Cartago, de Roma.
Y, sin embargo, no logra evitarlo.
Grande en su grandeza,
el hombre, piensa el ángel,
es insuperable en su servidumbre.

RAFAEL ARGULLOL

12-03-2013

Between five and six, every afternoon:
rush hour in London.
The Guardian Angel of cities
is surprised, like every other day,
by the precision of the mechanism.
Like puppets of an unseen puppeteer,
poor human beings
dash from here to there,
cast out of transparent Babel towers,
dragged by demons through fog and over tarmac,
thrust by the Furies down holes in the ground.
Every day the same rite is enacted:
the vertigo devouring creatures
hurriedly nowhere-bound.
The angel contemplates, gloomily,
how promptly the streets empty.
He has guarded men since Uruk was founded.
He has seen Nineveh, Carthage, Rome
rise and fall.
And can do nothing to prevent it.
In all his grandeur,
man, thinks the angel,
is utterly servile.

EFI CUBERO
(Granja de Torrehermosa, Badajoz, 1949)

LONDRES DESENFOCADO

> *focused at us, urging its noncompliance*
> *closer along the way we chose to go*
> JOHN ASHBERY

Basta sentir la atmósfera de Londres para abrigarte de las intemperies dejando que los pasos me conduzcan, a través de la niebla, atravesándolo.

Avanzar por sus calles como si me internara por un bosque de rótulos; árboles centenarios que soñaron a Dickens y miraron de frente los ojos de Virginia, los de Turner tal vez, agitando las ramas a su paso como si fueran olas de metálicas crestas abismáticas.

La ciudad, recelosa, nos muestra el laberinto mientras aguarda inevitables desmoronamientos.

Esta imagen palpable, y tan contradictoria, entre líneas sutiles habla a los ojos.

Su doble condición solo se alcanza en una suspensión del movimiento sobre el propio vacío.

No hay aquí auto indulgencia, sabe que buscas siempre algo que funde y funda. Apariencia y verdad: lo que puede rozarse y lo ilusorio.

Caminar por el borde de su acerado río es toda una experiencia.

Aguas turbias de un Támesis donde duerme sin paz el sueño del suicida.

O este frío luminoso de un lenguaje que nos hace temblar y arde a la vez, el cristal que traspasa soplado por el fuego que se templa detrás de los conceptos. La simultaneidad de una escala esencial de superficies que modula el silencio, y allá, al fondo del fondo, revelada en su fuerza, frágil y primitiva, la palabra quemada junto a Shelley, navegando tan limpia sobre el agua de Keats en desnudos exilios. Tan libre junto a Byron en las costas de Grecia al expirar con él y su destino.

EFI CUBERO

LONDON OUT OF FOCUS

> *focused at us, urging its noncompliance*
> *closer along the way we chose to go*
> JOHN ASHBERY

You only need to sense the atmosphere of London to wrap yourself up warm against the weather and I let my footsteps take me where they will through the mist, piercing it.

Making my way through the streets as if through a forest of signs: century-old trees that dreamt of Dickens and looked Virginia, perhaps Turner also, in the eyes, their branches shifting in their wake as if they were metallic crests of waves pulling them under.

The mistrustful city reveals its labyrinths meanwhile awaiting inevitable collapse.

This tangible paradoxical image speaks to the eye in subtle lines.

Its double condition is only achieved by a suspension of movement over the very abyss.

There is no self-indulgence here, be aware you are always seeking something that melts and builds. Appearance and truth: the concrete and the illusory.

Strolling along its steely river is something to experience.

Murky waters of a Thames where the suicide's dream sleeps fitfully.

Or this luminous cold of a language that makes us shiver and burns at the same time, that goes through glass blown by fire, tempered by concepts. The simultaneity of an essential scale of surfaces that silence modulates, and down there, in the depths of the depths, revealed in all its fragile primitive force, the word burnt with Shelley, sailing so cleanly on Keats's water in naked exiles. So free, with Byron on the Greek shore as it dies with him and with his destiny.

Los vectores pintados nos indican distintas direcciones a seguir.

Pero debo tomar la línea de autobuses 11 en King's Road. Desde la ventanilla, la abadía de Westminster donde duermen los nombres no olvidados, paso muy cerca de Downing Street donde el poder se ordena, y siguiendo a Whitehall, alzo los ojos hacia el yerto bronce de Trafalgar Square, y luego me detengo, duplicada e inmóvil, en acecho y alerta, impenetrable como la mirada o el objetivo que captó secuencias frente a las imposturas de lo que observamos.

Son los paralelepípedos de tantos laberintos como Londres contiene. Gestos en la saturación de un espacio marcado donde dejar la huella que nos ata. Escritura y sonido de los pasos, la construcción sonora donde auscultar los rastros de senderos borrados como una imaginada geografía que articula la propia realidad, hecha de vivo tránsito, o de esta incertidumbre que impide razonar frente a la mueca de nuestra calavera.

La experiencia se empapa de algún sueño. Detrás de la ventana alguien mira y también es observado. Un mundo abstracto de dolor y magia donde entender la misma complejidad del mundo, ser partícipe de la propia extrañeza, crear una metáfora del fragmento de un plano que se extiende y se dobla al infinito.

Aquí, en esta ciudad, se hallan las marcas de los encuentros y de los desencuentros, del azar y la vida que es inmortalizada en el instante mismo en el que los ojos creen descubrirla, o atraparla, como una realidad que es abstracción y que nunca podrá desvanecerse.

Es silencio y quietud; desasosiego que te permite ver los cambios más sutiles mientras la vida fluye inexorable.

Un reflejo que acecha en la mirada, en ella se demora, y así llega al final.

(Tal vez fuera el cansancio o la debilidad del andar mucho,

pero sentí que un vértigo de olvido me empujaba a la luz desde su torre).

The painted vectors show us different ways to go.

But I must catch the number 11 bus in King's Road. Out of the window, Westminster Abbey where sleep the unforgotten dead, I pass very close to Downing Street, where power is wielded, and in Whitehall I look up at the frozen bronze of Trafalgar Square, and then I halt, mirrored and motionless, alert, on the look-out, impenetrable as the gaze or the lens capturing footage of the impostures we observe.

They are the parallelepipeds of all the labyrinths London contains. Features in the saturation of a limited space where we leave the tracks that bind us. Writing and the sound of footsteps, a sound construction in which to listen to the heartbeat of lost trails as an imagined geography that articulates reality itself, made of living transit, or this uncertainty that prevents reasoning in the presence of our grimacing skulls.

Experience is soaked in some dream. Behind the window someone looks and is also observed. An abstract world of pain and magic in which to understand the very complexity of the world, participate in one's own alienation, create a metaphor from the fragment of a map that stretches and folds to infinity.

Here in this city are the imprints of encounters and missed encounters, of chance and life immortalised at the very moment the eyes believe they have caught or discovered, like an abstract reality that never can vanish.

It is silence and peace; a troubledness allowing one to perceive the most subtle changes while life continues its inexorable course.

A reflection dormant in the eyes, lingering there, and so arrives the end.

(It might have been weariness or weakness from so much walking,

but I felt a vertigo of oblivion pushing me towards the light up there in its tower).

JOAQUÍN SABINA
(Úbeda, Jaén, 1949)

BEGIN THE BEGUINE

Para el Nano, la Yuta y la María

London, hotel sin caspa, *fashion* en vena
con vistas a Hyde Park, pobre viejo rico,
ebrio de Samuel Johnson, Verlaine, Chirico,
bucanero del Támesis y del Sena.

Verde irlandés con asas por san Patricio,
mañanita *diumenge* de costalero,
los Bacon y los Turner, con aguacero,
acabarán sacando mi alma de quicio.

Por suerte mi bombín, cada madrugada,
goza de percha amiga donde colgarse,
nada como una Jime para olvidarse
del olvido que olvida tanta granada.

Con la frente marchita vuelvo a buscar
futuros imperfectos de mi pasado
con ganas de cobrarme lo malgastado
tan *begin the beguine* y vuelta a empezar.

¿Qué fue de aquellas niñas de la estación
que mordieron el polvo de las cunetas,
que endiosaron la tinta de los poetas,
que zurcieron un siete en mi corazón?

Estaba en pie la barra del Troubador,
los buses encarnados y las cabinas,
las *teenagers* en flor con anfetaminas
(qué *british* se conserva el conservador).

Con tanto agridulzor y neblina tanta,
prófugo de Carpanta regreso al foro

JOAQUÍN SABINA

BEGIN THE BEGUINE

For El Nano, la Yuta and la María

London, a smart hotel, mainlining *chic*
with views over The Park, poor old rich man,
drunk on Samuel Johnson, Verlaine, Chirico,
buccaneer of the Thames and of the Seine.

Irish green with handles, for St. Patrick,
a *costalero's*[i] Sunday morning,
the Bacons and Turners, in the pouring rain
are driving me out of my mind.

Luckily I hang my bowler hat
each night on a friendly hook,
nothing like a Sweet Jane to make you forget
the forgetting that forgets so much blood-letting.

With a wrinkled brow I'm back to look for
future imperfects from my past
with a longing to cash in my misspent youth
begin the beguine and here we go again.

Where are the girls of spring, ah where are they
who rolled with me in the ditches,
who glorified the poet's pen,
who sewed up my ragged heart?

The Troubadour bar was still standing,
incarnate and ruddy the buses and phone-boxes,
the teenagers high on speed
(how British the British always are).

With such bitter-sweetness and so much mist,
a refugee from hunger I return to the fray

---

[i] A *costalero* is a statue-bearer in the Holy Week processions.

como quien desespera del caño al coro,
muera la primavera, semana santa.

like someone who despairs from A to Z,
and Spring and Holy Week can go to hell.

LUIS SUÑÉN
(Madrid, 1951)

CAMDEN

Para María de Calonje y Mariano Antolín Rato

Sigues yendo por allí
porque te hace más joven
y por quererte todavía.
Son las mismas mujeres
de hace veinte años
y casi los mismos libros
—más ruido fuera y ya
no dejan estar dentro
con comida—.
Tus hijos dicen que
no entienden nada
y el concepto —digamos—
se ha quedado un poco
viejo. Pero algo tuviste y
hoy te lo das con cierta
plusvalía y hasta que
te veas en el
espejo del Toto
seguirás jugando a
que no ha pasado nada.
Luego echarás al canal
una flor por cada año
desde el primer día
y las verás correr por
el agua sucia,
y acariciar las tapias
del cementerio, y seguir vivas,
hasta hacerse basura.

LUIS SUÑÉN

CAMDEN

For María de Calonje and Mariano Antolín Rato

You still go down there
because it keeps your youth
and self-esteem alive.
The same women are there
as twenty years ago
and almost the same books –
more street-noise and now
you can't take food
in with you –.
Your children say
they just don't get it
and the concept, maybe,
has become a little
passé. But you had something and
today you have it still
in spades and until
you catch sight of yourself
in the mirror at Toto's
you'll go on pretending
everything is just the same.
Then you'll throw in the canal
one flower for every year
since the day you first came
and you'll watch them float away
on the dirty water
and rub against
the cemetery walls and stay
alive for a while,
until they become trash.

ÁNGELES MORA
(Rute, Córdoba, 1952)

EL HUECO DE LO VIVIDO

> *El río, la calle más larga de Londres...*
> ANNE PERRY

Y tras decir adiós despedimos la tarde.
Desde entonces un río
arrastra para siempre entre sus aguas turbias
aquel trozo de vida que quisimos guardar
en una imagen quieta.

Una foto pretende ser testigo del pasado,
de una tarde fugaz,
de un instante de luz.
No es lo que más me importa:
la verdadera foto ha quedado en el aire.
La imagen que más hiere
está pasando siempre, otra y la misma,
repitiéndose en mí,
igual que el Támesis escribe sin cesar
el corazón de Londres.

He vuelto del viaje y sin embargo
no regresé del todo,
algo me dejé atrás y algo me traje
que no entró en la maleta.

No me duele esta foto con su luz,
con su tarde brillando por mis ojos
y los tuyos, me duele aquel instante eterno
que no se fija ni se va,
aquel momento nuestro para siempre:
tú y yo, el río
y sus aguas revueltas.
El tiempo
corriendo con el día entrenublado
y el leve azul del norte.

ÁNGELES MORA

THE HOLE IN EXPERIENCE

> *The river, London's longest street...*
> ANNE PERRY

And after saying goodbye we took leave of the afternoon.
Since that day a river
forever in its turbid waters bears away
that bit of life we wished to preserve
in a fixed image.

A photograph claims to be a witness of the past,
of a fleeting afternoon,
of a moment of light.
That isn't what matters most to me:
the real photo remains in the air.
The most painful image
is always happening, different and the same,
over and over in me,
as the Thames is always writing
London's heart.

I'm back home from my travels, yet
not completely home,
I left something behind and brought something home
which didn't fit in the suitcase.

This photo with its light doesn't cause me pain,
with its afternoon shining out of my eyes
and out of yours, what causes me pain is that eternal moment
which neither stays nor leaves,
that moment ours forever:
you and me, the river
and its churning waters.
Time
racing by with the clouds
and the light blue Northern sky.

JAVIER VIRIATO
(Zaragoza, 1955)

ATARDECER DE HIELOS

Suenan granuladas gotas en la tarde fría como agua
La lámpara tiñe su aura de amarillo, no llueve nada
¿notas que el sonido es más frío, más metal que árbol río?
solo al palpar la profundidad de mi silencio me altero
aunque ya la estufa cubre de reflejos rojos la alfombra

¿Pero qué es la ignorancia, qué el vaciamiento repleto?

¿Ámbito de incendios, paisaje de arenas, noche de infierno?
Tu cuerpo como una flor, como una playa tu cuerpo entero.

¿El juego es algo vacío o el más grande, el más pleno
a
  c T
   o?

Vacío, al fin.

Mareo, un garabato, a veces, ola un estallido
(he salido a mear y la noche se ha presentado las músicas se han agitado, el cielo sobre Londres arde)
Pero al juego al que yo me refiero se juega solo o si acaso
                       un objeto
                       un gato
                           duerme
                           escucha
                           pestañea
                         extendido en
                         la colcha blanca
                     una ausencia

Tres hojas al vuelo de mis pensamientos
La soledad alegre como aventura
     Tu nube se desliza ante mis ojos

JAVIER VIRIATO

NIGHTFALL AND HAIL

Granules clatter in the night as cold as water
The lamp stains its aura yellow, it doesn't rain
Can you tell that the sound is colder, more metallic than river tree?
only when I feel the depth of my silence do I shiver
though the stove casts its red light on the carpet

But what is ignorance, what utter emptying?

The reach of fire, sandscape, infernal night?
Your body like a flower, like a beach your whole body.

Is the game an empty thing or the greatest, most complete
a
  c
    T?

Empty, finally.

Dizziness, a scribble, sometimes, a wave crash
(I went out to pee and the night showed up the musics jangled, the sky over London is burning)
But the game I refer to is played alone or just maybe
                an object
              a cat
                  sleeps
                  listens
                  blinks
                  lying on
                    the white coverlet
              an absence

Three leaves blow through my thoughts
Loneliness like a joyful adventure
    Your cloud slides before my eyes

			entre mis dedos
Te juro voy a contarte muchas historias
				sí, muchas mentiras.

                    between my fingers
I swear I'll tell you many stories
                    yes, many lies.

JAVIER PÉREZ WALIAS
(Plasencia, Cáceres, 1960)

UN HOMBRE SE HA DETENIDO EN ALBERT BRIDGE

Un río de hombres.
De regreso, cruzamos el puente.
Un hombre se ha detenido. El corazón de este hombre, que observa a
      otros hombres pasar
con sus rostros
vaciados
en plomo,
flota
como flotan los pájaros.
Los ojos de este hombre, que observa a otros hombres pasar con sus
      rostros vaciados
en plomo,
se alejan despacio buscando otra luz más intensa
en la tenue silueta
del cielo.
El bullicio ámbar de un mirlo se atenúa
de golpe.
Este hombre, que observa a otros hombres pasar con sus rostros vaciados
      en plomo, que se ha detenido en el centro
del puente,
ha fijado sus ojos
en una pálida brizna
de luz.
Este hombre acostumbra a mirarse
a sí mismo.
Lo he visto algunas mañanas de invierno paseando con calma por
      Battersea Park. Lo he visto sentado
en un banco,
junto a la extraña pagoda del parque,
limpiando
el fruto de una espiga —en paz— o comulgando
el pan
de un ángel
caído.

JAVIER PÉREZ WALIAS

A MAN STOPPED ON ALBERT BRIDGE

A river of men.
On the way back, we cross the bridge.
A man has stopped on the bridge. The heart of this man observing other
        men passing by,
with their vacant
leaden
faces,
flutters
as birds flutter.
The eyes of this man observing other men passing by, with their vacant leaden
faces,
drift slowly into the distance seeking a different intenser light
in the faint silhouette
of the sky.
The amber commotion of a blackbird fades
suddenly.
This man observing other men passing by, with their vacant leaden faces,
        who has stopped in the middle
of the bridge,
now contemplates
a pallid blade
of light.
This man has the habit
of observing himself
I've seen him some winter mornings strolling through Battersea Park.
        I've seen him sitting
on a bench,
by the peculiar pagoda in the park,
cleaning the grains
of an ear of wheat – peaceably – or savouring
the communion-wafer
of a fallen
angel.

En la puerta del templo, le he visto dejar sus sandalias. He sentido sus
        pasos descalzos, sus pies descalzos
sobre la hierba
caminando desnudos. Su presencia
no era
la de un hombre
común.
El corazón de este hombre, que observa a otros hombres pasar por el
        puente con sus rostros
vaciados
en plomo, desanda
el camino.
De regreso. Juntos vadeamos el río
por Albert
bridge.

[Londres, septiembre de 2013]

I have seen him leave his sandals at the temple door. I've heard his unshod
        footsteps, his unshod feet
on the grass
walking barefoot. His presence
was that
of a man
out of the common way.
The heart of this man observing other men crossing the bridge,
        with their vacant
leaden faces, retraces
its steps.
Returns. Together we ford the river
over Albert
Bridge.

[London, September 2013]

CARLOS MARZAL
(Valencia, 1961)

LA LLUVIA EN REGENT'S PARK

Debe de estar lloviendo en Regent's Park.
Y una suave neblina hará que se extravíe
la hierba en el perfil del horizonte,
los robles a lo lejos, las flores, los arriates.
Pausada, compasiva, descenderá la lluvia
hoy sobre el corazón de la ciudad,
su angustia, su estruendo,
sobre el mínimo infierno inabarcable
de cada pobre diablo.
Igual que aquella tarde en la que fui feliz,
igual que aquella lluvia
que me purificó, caritativa.

En las horas peores,
cuando el desierto avanza,
y no hay robles, ni hay hierba, cuando pienso
que no saldré jamás del laberinto,
y siento el alma sucia,
y el cuerpo, que se arrastra,
cobarde, entre la biografía,
la lluvia, en el recuerdo, me limpia, me acaricia,
me vuelve a hacer aún digno,
aún merecedor
de algún día de gloria de la vida.
La amable, la misericordiosa,
la dulce lluvia inglesa.

CARLOS MARZAL

RAIN IN REGENT'S PARK

It must be raining in Regents Park.
And a soft mist will make the grass
lose its way on the horizon line,
the oaks in the distance, the flowers, the parterres.
Slow, compassionate, the rain will fall
today over the city's heart,
its anguish, its turmoil,
over the minimal immense hell
of every poor devil.
Just like that afternoon when I was happy,
just like that rain
that purified me, solacing.

In the terrible hours,
when the desert encroaches,
and there are no oaks, no grass, when I think
I am trapped forever in the maze,
and my soul feels soiled,
and my body feels sluggish
and, cowardly, caught inside my life,
the rain I remember washes me clean,
caresses me, makes me worthy again,
deserving even
one of life's glorious days,
beneath the kind and merciful
soft English rain.

EDUARDO MOGA
(Barcelona, 1962)

[CASAS, LACERACIONES...]

Casas, laceraciones.
Casas enclavadas en el suelo,
en el sueño,
                sobrevoladas por amatistas
y eclipses,
             sacudidas por espasmos
de penumbra.
              La puerta roja,
la tiniebla roja
              de un comedor,
la escamosa proliferación de la arcilla,
que es, pese a su cuerpo multitudinario,
un solo cuerpo, una agrupación arbórea de ímpetu
y derramamiento.
           Ventanas,
pupilas inversas, pasadizos
a una intimidad lábil —una tetera, una camisa sin planchar,
              alguien que lee un libro—,
heladas por la lluvia
y la indiferencia.
           Puertas, ventanas,
sucesos entre muros
o entre nubes,
         paredes que se persiguen
entre castaños, o que escapan
como criaturas lentas,
              alarmadas por el sol,
deseosas de sol, pero invadidas
de silencio,
       casas huérfanas a cuyas
fachadas, en las que se alinean las columnas
y la hipocresía,
           acuden los cables de la electricidad
como enjambres filiformes,

EDUARDO MOGA

HOUSES, LACERATIONS…

Houses, lacerations.
Houses set deep in the ground,
set deep in dream,
     overflown by amethysts,
eclipses,
  shaken by penumbral
spasms.
   The red door,
red darkness
   of a dining-room,
scaly proliferation of clay,
which is, for all its myriad body,
one single body, an arboreal cluster
of force and spillage.
     Windows,
reverse pupils, passages
to a labile intimacy – a teapot, an unironed shirt,
someone reading –,
frozen by rain
and indifference.
    Doors, windows,
events between walls,
or between clouds,
walls chasing each other
through chestnut trees, or fleeing
like heavy creatures,
     alarmed by the sun,
longing for sun, but invaded
by silence,
   orphaned houses to whose
facades, on which are aligned
columns and hypocrisy,
     come electric cables
like threaded swarms,

casas en las profundidades de lo visible,
en las que reconozco toda álgebra y
toda turbiedad, pero cuyo reconocimiento
no altera la certeza de que son edificios intangibles,
seres que ni atormentan ni aman,
                              de que su raíz es la distancia,
de que la argamasa y las pizarras y las chimeneas
                                        y las moquetas
y los seres que las habitan —uno de los cuales soy yo—
son entelequias
o cadáveres.
              Primrose Mansions.
Prímula: la primera que florece en la estación:
su amarillo lánguido tiene prisa por morir.
Y *Rosebery Villa*: el escaramujo, un arañazo de óxido,
una eclosión imperfecta
                    en la perfección de la rosa.
Estos edificios no significan nada:
su solidez es incorpórea,
              como la levedad en que perecen.
Al acercarme a ellos, mi piel se contagia
de su insuficiencia: también yo me empequeñezco;
también mi nombre se arruina, como la pintura
que deserta de sus muros
vegetales.
          Estas casas no están, aunque las vea
cada día,
aunque cada día, al salir de casa, se me aparezcan
con la gravidez de algo concluyente,
                              de algo como un precipicio
o una tumba: verlas cada día es la mejor prueba
de su inexistencia.
                Y tampoco yo estoy: verlas cada día
demuestra también mi desaparición.
                              Allí, una cabeza de ciervo.
El ciervo es blanco, y, como algunas pinturas antiguas,
parece mirarme desde dondequiera que lo mire yo.
Los callejones, macilentos,
se han enamorado de la basura.

houses deep inside the visible,
in which I recognise all algebra,
all darkness, but this recognition
doesn't affect the conviction they are intangible
structures, entities that neither torture nor love,
                                        whose root is distance,
whose mortar, slates, and chimneys
                              and carpets,
and whose inhabitants – and I am one of them –
are fantasies
or corpses.
             Primrose Mansions.
Primrose: first flower of spring:
its languid yellow hastening to death.
And *Roseberry Villa:* the rose-hip, a scratch of rust,
flawed bloom
                     in the perfection of the rose.
These buildings have no meaning:
their solidity yields,
                     like their light mortality.
As I approach them, my skin prickles
with their lack: I too shrink;
my name too decays, like the paint
peeling from their vegetal
walls.
     These houses don't exist, though I see them
every day,
though every day, when I come out of my house, there they are,
pregnant, conclusive
                  as a precipice
or a tomb: seeing them every day is proof positive
of their non-existence.
                    And I don't exist either: seeing them every day
is proof too of my own vanishing.
                            Over there, a deer's head.
It's a white deer, and, like some old paintings,
it seems to be looking at me no matter where I stand.
The haggard alleyways
have fallen in love with their garbage.

La basura es pulcra como la luna,
se corrompe como la luna,
dispara las alarmas de los coches
y de las casas,
como la luna.
   andra
   ue:
así reza un rótulo callejero: un nombre amputado,
como el mío,
como la luna.
    Estas casas son trincheras inmateriales.
Las ventanas, párpados,
muñones,
se revisten de escayola
y mansedumbre; sin alterarse,
se resquebrajan; y, enteladas de ocaso,
convocan a la opacidad.
     Las ventanas se dividen
en cuadrángulos, como esta celda con televisión por cable y suelo
radiante
en la que me abismo
en mí
   para ver lo que rehúye la mirada,
lo que se ofrece desnudamente a la mirada,
y articular cuanto carece de sustancia,
       porque carece de amor,
porque no pronuncia palabras
     ni se desgaja del olvido,
porque se asienta en una estructura que es
un coágulo
   y un desprendimiento.
Alexandra Avenue dice otro rótulo.
Avenida: desbordamiento de pasos que no
permanecen,
caudal de formas que discrepan
de la muerte,
   pero destinadas a morir.
Aunque no aquí.
    Aquí cada jamba,

The garbage is as dainty as the moon,
rots like the moon,
sets off car-alarms
and house-alarms,
like the moon.
    andra
    ue:
declares a street-sign: an amputated name,
like mine,
like the moon.
    These houses are unsolid trenches.
Windows, eyelids,
stumps,
wear stucco
and meekness; they crack
insensibly; and, wrapped in sunset,
invoke opacity.
    The windows are divided into fours,
as is this cell with cable and underfloor
heating, in which
I sink into the abyss of myself
      to see
what the eye refuses,
what shows itself naked to the eye,
and to put into words all that lacks substance,
        because it lacks love
because it is mute,
    oblivious,
because it is set in a structure that is
a clot in the blood
    a detached retina.
Alexandra Avenue says another street-sign.
Avenue: flood of fugitive
footsteps,
spate of forms denying
death,
  but destined anyway to die.
Though not here.
    Here every doorjamb,

cada espacio cimentado es un simulacro
de fuga,
   cada ser es otra cosa,
otro farolillo moribundo,
otra rosa o primavera
junto a los desechos de las obras,
      a las sillitas de niño abandonadas,
o los yonquis que languidecen entre paraguas desmadejados,
o los tablones que se pudren al sol acuoso
del otoño.
   Hasta los perros se resisten a ser perros,
y actúan como máquinas
      o nulidades.
Nada hay aquí que me exonere de la nada;
no hay metáforas en las que guarecerme;
no hay luz, ni compasión, ni úteros, ni soportales.
La perversión es sinuosa como las fachadas,
y así se dirige a su fin: como una flecha curva,
      como una flecha que no duda.
La vegetación que asoma en algunos zaguanes
duele como una mano cortada,
como una ofensa
entre carcajadas.
   (Pero las carcajadas son frías,
como el oro de los bejucos,
como los cirros que se malignizan al atardecer,
como el mar que late lejos,
     o que no existe).
Y yo, en el cuadrángulo.
El cuadrángulo: donde conviven la comodidad
y la herrumbre,
y el silencio es rojo, como las tapias
y las amapolas,
y los ascensores trasiegan sordomudos,
y los perros siempre ladran, aunque sepan quién eres.
(Los perros lo saben mejor que las personas).
El cuadrángulo, donde el silencio
es una navaja que recorre la piel
sobrecogida y solo la abandona

    each cemented space is a semblance
of escape,
      each creature is something other,
another little dying lamp,
another rose or spring
with the builders waste
and the thrown-out child-chairs,
or the junkies lolling between sprawled umbrellas
or the planks rotting in the watery
autumn sun.
      Even the dogs refuse to be dogs
and act like machines
        or nullities.
Nothing here exempts me from the void;
there are no metaphors for refuge;
there is no light or pity, womb or lintel.
Perversion is sinuous like these facades,
and goes for its target: like a curved arrow,
          decisive as an arrow.

The plants in the hallways
hurt like a severed hand,
like a laughing
insult.
   (But the laughter is cold
like the golden climbing plants,
like the cirrus's malignancy at dusk,
like the sea lapping miles away,
       or nowhere.)
And I within the quadrangle.
The quadrangle: where comfort and rust
co-exist,
and the silence is red, like the walls
and the poppies,
and the deaf-mute lifts ascend,
and the dogs always bark, though they know who you are.
(They know you better than the people do.)
The quadrangle, where silence
is a knife drawn over the startled
skin, only ceasing when it has stripped it

cuando se ha despojado de toda fraternidad,
y la esperanza, una prímula
pronta a morir
        junto a la entrada
del aparcamiento.
El andamio que veo, desde esta ventana
a la que se reduce el mundo, es solo otra escalera
al no ser. Nada quedará
de su ascensión.
              Andamio, *scaffold*, significa también patíbulo.
Esta entereza, esta urdimbre de sílice,
esta proyección tubular
de lo que es masa y oquedad,
no conduce sino a la desmemoria,
y la desmemoria me ahoga: lo que no comprendo,
no es; lo que niega,
no vive.
       ¿Me sostienen estos adoquines cansados, estos tabiques
como ceniza?
         ¿Me transfunden, con su marchita rectitud,
el pálpito, el centelleo
             de los pies que los han pisado
o la tibieza de las caricias que han sostenido?
¿Me incomoda la sangre que los jaspea
o solo su densidad extinta,
            el oro exánime de su noche?
¿O estoy yo cansado como ellos, tatuado por idénticos aguaceros,
desquiciado por el gravitar de los minutos?
No tengo vecinos, sino enemigos.
Yo no soy su vecino: también soy su enemigo.
                    Y el mío.

[YVON HOUSE Y TODO LO DEMÁS – 7 DE ENERO DE 2014]
Vivimos en un piso que se encuentra en un inmueble rehabilitado. Antes Yvon House —así se llama— era una fábrica, como tantos otros edificios del barrio. De hecho, casi todo el barrio era una zona industrial, que albergaba, por su proximidad con el río y los nudos ferroviarios del sur de Londres, almacenes, silos, factorías y muelles. Con el paso del tiempo y el crecimiento de la población, que empujaba esas amplias y destartaladas extensiones

of all humanity,
and hope, a primrose
soon to die
        beside the entrance
to the car-park.
The scaffolding I see, from this window
which is my little world, is only another stairway
to non-existence. Nothing will remain
from its flight.
        Scaffolding. Scaffold. Gibbet.
This platform, this warp of silica,
this tubular projection
of what is mass and hollow,
leads only to disremembering,
and I am choked with disremembering: what I don't
understand, is not; what it rejects
dies.
    Do these weary cobbles, these ashy partitions
sustain me?
        In their withered rectitude, do they transfuse
the heartbeat, the spark
        of the feet who have walked on them
or the warm hands that touched them?
Is it the flecks of blood disturb me,
or only their thick extinction,
        the lifeless blood of their night?
Or am I tired like them, tattooed by the same rain,
maddened by the whirring of the clock.
I don't have neighbours, but enemies.
I'm not their neighbour; but I too am their enemy.
        And my own.

[YVON HOUSE AND THE REST OF IT – JANUARY 7TH 2014]
We're living in a flat in a conversion. Yvon House, like so many other buildings in the neighbourhood, was once a factory. In fact, the whole district, almost, was an industrial zone which, because it was near the river and the South London railway network, was made up of warehouses, silos, works and wharves. As time passed and the population grew, this vast and shabby apparatus of manufacture was pushed further and further out of the city – it's

fabriles hacia unos confines cada vez más alejados del centro de la ciudad —es sorprendente pensar lo cerca que quedaban del corazón del mundo, simbolizado por el edificio del Parlamento—, el espacio que ocupaban se ha destinado a viviendas y equipamientos públicos. No sé qué se fabricaba o almacenaba aquí. Sí, que la reconstrucción ha sido cuidadosa, y que la planta, cuadrangular, y el ladrillo original del edificio se han preservado. Este ladrillo inglés no es tan oscuro como lo pintan, sino que cubre una extensa gama de tonos rojizos: a veces, roza el granate; otras es ocre, incluso rubio. Durante muchos siglos, ha sido el humo de las fábricas el que lo ha tiznado hasta casi la negrura; ahora son el de los tubos de escape y el de la contaminación que genera la actividad humana los responsables de que se oscurezca. Desde nuestro comedor, en el que sobreviven también tres grandes ventanas de la antigua factoría, se ven, muy próximas, las casas de enfrente. La calle es estrecha y su nombre no resulta demasiado eufónico: Warriner Gardens. Se pronuncia guorriner (o guarriner, aún no hemos conseguido averiguarlo) y no tiene jardines, salvo que queramos considerar jardines los escuchimizados arriates antepuestos a algunas casas. Pero esto es normal aquí: nuestra dirección es Alexandra Avenue, que no es una avenida, y en Warriner Gardens no hay jardines. A veces me quedo mirando por la ventana lo que hacen los vecinos de enfrente. La curiosidad es un impulso natural del ser humano: cuando recae, por ejemplo, en esas extrañas floraciones que asoman en el microscopio, nos proporciona la penicilina; cuando se aplica a la vida de los vecinos, da para una película como La ventana indiscreta *o para una entrada en un blog. Lo cierto es que me siento una mezcla de James Stewart y Henri-Frédéric Amiel. Siempre me ha llamado la atención en Inglaterra el contraste entre la importancia que se otorga a la intimidad de cada cual, a la privacidad de los ciudadanos, y la despreocupación con que muchos de esos ciudadanos muestran esa misma vida privada a los demás. Las casas que tenemos delante son antiguas, estrechas, modestas. No viven ricos en ellas. En muchas las cortinas nunca están corridas. En una siempre veo niños en pijama, una madre que plancha y un abuelo sentado en un sofá, que bebe de una taza. Los niños me miran también por la ventana, y deben de pensar que en mi piso las cortinas no están nunca corridas, y que alguien muy alto y con barba, que bebe de una taza, les está espiando. Ayer, cuando estaba de vigía, pasó el cartero, vestido de rojo. No sé si Correos se habrá privatizado ya: así lo había decidido el gobierno. El otrora legendario servicio de correos británico será ahora una empresa más, que honrará exclusivamente el principio del lucro. El cartero estuvo hablando un buen rato con una vecina, que parecía describirle, con gestos, un paquete que no había llegado. Mientras ambos dialogaban, se*

strange to think how close it used to be to the heart of the capital, as represented by the Houses of Parliament – and the hole it left given over to housing and services. I don't know what was manufactured or stored here. The conversion has certainly been carried out sympathetically, the quadrangular footprint of the original building and its brickwork have been kept as they were. This English brick isn't as dark as people have described it. It comes in a wide range of reds: sometimes dark crimson, at times ochre, even ruby-red. For centuries it was blackened by factory smoke; now it's car-exhausts and general pollution that darken it. From our dining room, which has three long windows from the old factory, you can see, close-up, the houses opposite. The street is narrow with an ugly name: Warriner Gardens. We're not sure how to pronounce Warriner, as we haven't heard anyone say it out loud, and there aren't any gardens, unless you count the scant flowerbeds in front of some of the houses. But that's normal here: our address is Alexandra Avenue, which isn't an avenue, just as Warriner Gardens is gardenless. Sometimes I stand at the window seeing what the neighbours are doing. Curiosity is a natural human impulse: when it lights on strange blooms in the microscope, for instance, it discovers penicillin.; when it observes the lives of neighbours it can give rise to a film like Rear Window or ideas for a blog-entry. It's true I often feel like a cross between James Stewart and Henri-Frédéric Amiel. I'm always struck by the contrast between the emphasis on the individual's right to privacy in England and the relaxed way they leave their private lives open to the gaze of others. The houses opposite are old, narrow, modest. The people who live there aren't rich. In many of them the curtains are never closed. In one I always see children in pyjamas, a mother ironing, and a granddad sitting on a sofa, drinking out of a mug. The children too watch me from their window, and they probably think the curtains of my flat are always open, and that a very tall man with a beard, drinking out of a mug, is spying on them. Yesterday, when I was on the watch, the postman passed by, wearing red. I wonder if the Post Office has already been privatised. The once legendary British GPO will soon be a business like any other, only concerned with making money. The postman stood talking with a neighbour for some time. She seemed to be describing to him a mislaid parcel, with accompanying gestures. While the two of them were talking, a woman came out of the house next door. She was wearing a white dressing-gown and slippers, and drinking from a mug. Here we all drink out of mugs: it's a characteristic, a differential, but not like the differentials in car-engines I think. I wasn't able to ascertain why she had come out: she stood for a few moments in her doorway, glanced at her neighbour and the postman, then up and down the street, and went back indoors. Presiding over the scene

abrió la puerta de al lado y salió una señora en bata blanca y zapatillas de baño, que bebía de una taza. Aquí todos bebemos de taza: beber de taza es un rasgo diferencial, aunque nunca he sabido muy bien en qué se diferencia este «diferencial» del que hay en los motores de los coches. No pude descubrir por qué salió: estuvo unos segundos en la puerta, miró discretamente a la vecina y al cartero, echó otro vistazo a la calle, y volvió adentro. Presidiendo la escena, dos coches aparcados: un mini, rojo con listas blancas, y un bentley morado, antiguo pero fulgurante: el amor por los coches de los ingleses no conoce límites y se manifiesta en cualquier barrio, en cualquier rincón. Por la tarde, Á. y yo salimos a pasear por el barrio y tomamos por Warriner Gardens. Al lado de nuestro edificio hay otro semejante, aunque mucho más bonito. Es también una antigua fábrica, pero aquí la remodelación ha sido más lujosa, casi barroca, con puentecillos metálicos que conectan las diferentes galerías de los pisos, luces integradas en las paredes, plantas ornamentales y una oscuridad de terciopelo, con incrustaciones doradas: se llama Mandeville Courtyard. Algo más allá, distinguimos un negocio: McKinney & Co., que, por su nombre y la tipografía empleada, creímos una empresa de whisky. Nos defraudó comprobar que solo era una lavandería. Como para recordarnos los placeres que nos habíamos perdido, pasaron a nuestro lado en aquel momento dos gordos tatuados, descamisados y felices, que parloteaban en un inglés impenetrable y sorbían jubilosamente de sendas latas de Guinness. A esa hora, los vecinos ya no salían de casa. La oscuridad empapaba las fachadas. En casi todas las entradas se amontonaban los cubos de basura. Quizá alguien, desde alguna ventana, nos vería pasar, indolentemente, por la calle, y se preguntaría qué hacían aquellos dos mirando las fachadas oscuras de las casas, con el frío que hacía.

were two parked cars: a Mini, red with white stripes, and a maroon Bentley, ancient but dazzling: the English love of cars knows no limits, you can see evidence of it everywhere, round every corner. In the evening, A. and I went out for a walk round the block, and we walked up Warriner Gardens. Next to our building is one much the same, but prettier. It too is a former factory, but here the conversion has been more elaborate, almost baroque, with little metal bridges connecting floor to floor, lights set into the walls, decorative plantings, and a velvety darkness inlaid with gold: it's name is Mandeville Courtyard. A little further on, we could see a shop-sign: McKinney & Co. The lettering and name made us think of a whisky firm, so we were disappointed to discover it was only a launderette. As if to remind us of forgotten pleasures, two fat tattooed men came by us then, shirts off and merry, bantering in uncatchable English and slurping cans of Guinness. It was late, and the neighbours had all gone inside. A darkness soaked the facades. There were dustbins at almost every gate. Maybe someone at one of the windows saw us wander by, and wondered what those two were doing looking up at the houses, when it was so cold out.

MANUEL VILAS
(Barbastro, Huesca, 1962)

LONDRES

Hubiera deseado quedar allí por siempre.
Encontrar una obligación menor
que me diera, sin penas,
el justo dinero para vivir.
No regresar a España nunca más,
y vivir anónimo
como un rey en su inventado sueño de destierro.
Asistir a la ópera, bajo aquellos oscuros
corredores del metro.
Y saber para siempre que ningún rostro humano
me sería penosamente familiar.
Y perder la conciencia de la lengua
y con ella, tal en sutil venganza,
la de la poesía.
No escribir más, no tener amigos,
y cuidar raramente
de mi plácido y sobrio, noble jardín inglés,
vigilar mi casa y ocupar mi tiempo
en el libre y claro amor a mí mismo.
Alcanzar una honorable vejez,
después de muchos años,
y la dulce pérdida de mi estirpe,
mi nombre y mi memoria en umbroso rincón
de cualquier cementerio londinense,
allí donde jamás me encontrase el destino
que me consume, y dar esquinazo al tiempo,
a dios, al diablo y a la humanidad entera.

MANUEL VILAS

LONDON

I could have wished to stay there always.
Find an untaxing job
which would provide me
with just enough to live on.
And never ever go back to Spain,
live anonymously
like a king in an invented dream of exile.
Go to the opera, down the dark
corridors of the underground.
Be sure of never seeing
a painfully familiar face.
Lose my sense of language
and with it, like a subtle vengeance,
my sense of poetry.
Write no more, have no friends,
and cultivate occasionally
my calm and sober, noble English garden,
take care of my house and occupy my time
in free and bright self-love.
Reach an honourable old-age,
after many years,
and the sweet mislaying of my lineage,
my name and my memory in a shady corner
of some London cemetery,
where I won't be tracked down by the fate
that consumes me and can give the slip to time,
to god and the devil, to the entire human race.

JUAN CARLOS MARSET
(Albacete, 1963)

LABERINTO (fragmento)

(...)
Tú salías temprano
a la estación de Parsons Green,
con tu almuerzo dispuesto
para el ceremonial
de lo crudo y crujiente,
lo blando y resistente, lo que cede
y al romper se deshace o se defiende,
lo húmedo secado,
lo seco humedecido,
los ocultos aromas
y ligues que desprende
al diente comedido lo sabido,
según inventariemos o inventemos
las secretas recetas de la Perla,
la perla de las perlas que aprendí
y que perdí al verla,
para la hora libre de jornada
que a tu sabor reposa
en el ameno huerto de los plátanos
del monstruo de Saint James
hispánico y de Londres
en tu plaza emplazada.
Yo me quedaba en Fulham
con el cuerpo alterado por el viaje
y todavía el tiempo
contraído a tu cuerpo.
Salía a Londres
soñoliento a primera hora del día
y ciertamente vi
el laberinto donde siempre
me he encontrado saliendo:
el laberinto de mis laberintos
de infinitas salidas sin entrada.

JUAN CARLOS MARSET

LABYRINTH *(fragment)*

(…)
You left early
for Parsons Green station
with your lunch prepared
for the ceremony
of raw and crunchy,
of soft and hard, what gives way
and when it snaps falls to bits or resists,
the moist gone dry,
the dry moistened,
the hidden aromas
and associations
the known affords
to the leisurely tooth,
as we would list or invent
the secret recipes of the Pearl,
the pearl of pearls I apprehended
and lost on sight,
for the lunch-hour
that for your taste reposes
among the pleasant plane-trees
of monstrous Spanish
Saint James and of London
in your place in your square.
I stayed in Fulham
my body depleted by the journey
and time still
shrunk to your body.
I came out into London
sleepy in the first light
and certainly I saw
the labyrinth where always
I met myself coming out:
the labyrinth of my labyrinths

Se sale adonde vayas,
porque ni entrar a Londres ni de Londres
salir se puede (…).
No por haber entrado
sino por no salir en cada intento
de Londres más que a Londres.
No juegan las palabras, no es el verbo
el riesgo, ni es el sueño que tenemos,
no es la falta de empleo
ni de empeño: es la falta
para salir de entrada,
la falta de salida para entrar.
Es la *falta* asfaltada
por la que recurrentes recorremos
Londres sin encontrar
el paso para entrar a la ciudad
de nuestro encuentro,
en Londres la ciudad que nos perdemos
al no salir de Londres sin perdernos.
Salimos tantas veces sin entrar
a Londres que al fin fue
morada prolongada
de un volver a salir
en este laberinto umbilical
sin comienzo ni fin
(…). Viéndote
camino de tu jaula
dorada sobre el Mall,
urdía consentido tu rescate
como un donjuán burlando leyes
lelas, leyendas rejas, relajadas
reglas del deber ser
y no del ser deudor.
Vivimos en el rito de la Sierpe,
en el tiempo del precio y del desprecio,
preciosos y precisos
por igual. La memoria
de Croce en un recodo
napolitano en Chelsea se cruzó

with myriad exits and no entrance.
Wherever you go you go out
because you can't either get into London
or leave London (…)
Not for having entered
but for not exiting each time you try
from London rather than into London.
This isn't a paradox, the words
aren't the problem, nor how sleepy we are,
nor is it idleness
or effort: it's the lack
of an exit to begin with,
the lack of an exit to go into.
It's *lack* tarmacked:
we go round and round
London without finding
an entrance to the city
of our encounter,
in London the city we miss
when we can't leave London without getting lost.
We left London so many times
without entering it that it became
a stay prolonged
by a re-exiting
in this umbilical labyrinth
with no beginning and no end
(…) Seeing you
on the way to your golden
cage on The Mall,
I serenely plotted your rescue
like a Don Juan laughing at foolish laws,
grid-legends, barred windows, relaxed
rules about our debt to life
and not about the debts we owe.
We live in the rite of the Serpent,
in the age of cost and contempt,
precious and precise
at once. The memory
of Croce on a Neapolitan

con la imaginación de irrealidades
reales para Blake y para Milton
más que las irreales realidades
del laberinto mundo en que vivimos.
(…) Cuando a Londres salíamos,
cada gesto mostraba
el mito de las gestas sucesivas.
Un anuncio de Nike
el verdugo de Marsias,
el saludo de un chef cuchillo
en mano el sacrificio
del hijo de Abraham. El diapasón
del día se extendía al desviarnos
por barrios divertidos
o aviesamente resentidos,
poblados por residuos coloniales
danzando su acechanza,
dominando el idioma de su de-
nominador común:
el carcelero idioma
del lenguaje tribal atribulado
que al nombre da
lo que le quita el nombre.
Ecos de Mallarmé
en el exilio de la voz
y en el criollo Walcott
que en Londres denunció
del canto la redada
que al enredarse
en la red del lenguaje reo escapa
cárcel que huyendo habita
el liberado pájaro sin red.
En Hampstead escuchamos
del ruiseñor de Keats
el canto que perdura
en *terredad*, compuesto
por Eugenio Montejo
en otras partituras
de parturienta voz.

corner of Chelsea came up against
the imagining of unrealities
real for Blake and for Milton
more than the unreal realities
of the labyrinth world we live in.
(...) When we went out to London,
every face demonstrated
the myth of consecutive triumph.
A Nike advertisement
the executioner of Marsyas,
the greeting of a chef knife
in hand the sacrifice
of Abraham's son. The day's
diapason widened as we wandered
through quaint neighbourhoods
or viciously resentful ones,
populated by colonial residue
dancing their ambush,
speaking the language of the-
ir common denominator:
the jailer language
of the troubled tribal dialect
that gives a name
to what robs its name.
Echoes of Mallarmé
in the exile of the voice
and in the Creole Walcott
who in London railed against
the trawl of song
that becoming entangled
in the net of the culpable language escapes
the prison which, fleeing, the freed
bird inhabits unentangled.
In Hampstead we heard
the song of Keats's nightingale
still alive in *Terredad*
by Eugenio Montejo
in new melodies
from a voice giving birth.

Y al respirar la rosa del jardín,
la máscara de Keats nos recordó
con sus ojos cerrados viendo
y sus labios callados advirtiendo
la muerte que se pasa contemplando
la vida que se viene tan callando.
(…) En el oscuro espejo
de la piedra Rosetta de tu oficio,
al ver tus labios rosa entre las rosas
salvajes del rosal
salvado del rosario
de Londres sin entrada,
al decirnos la fuga decidimos.
El rastro de la rosa
por los parques trazados
como selvas domadas perseguimos,
y el ruido derruido
del ruiseñor en ríos comerciales
donde los pordioseros de otro tiempo
hoy son turistas que por dioses ser
en lugar de pedir limosna os dan
divisas, divas dádivas, propinas
y lástima al pasar.
Risas del ruiseñor y de la rosa
nos trajeron al Támesis,
río que suena a musa
hija de Mnemosyne,
la madre memoriosa
de los únicos días en el día.
Tan cerca de la puerta
morada nuestra
en la calle del Monstruo,
del Támesis al paso
el paso acompasamos.
En Bishop's Park un plátano
hispánico de Londres
nos sugirió las fuentes donde surge
el pasado británico
afluente de tu Rhin,

And as we breathed in the scent
of the rose in the garden
Keats's mask reminded us,
with its closed seeing eyes
and its silent lips warning,
of death spent contemplating
life which stealthily comes closer to us.
(…) In the dark mirror
of the Rosetta stone of your occupation,
seeing your rosy lips in the wild
roses on the rose-bush
saved from the rosary
of unenterable London,
when we spoke of escape we made our minds up.
We followed the trail of the rose
through the laid-out parks,
like tamed jungles,
and the ruined sound
of the nightingale down rivers of commerce,
where the beggars of old
are tourists now who, godlike as they are,
don't beg for alms but hand over
cash, lordly gifts, tips, as they pass by,
we pity them.
The nightingale's, the rose's laughter
brought us down to the Thames,
a river that sounds like a muse
daughter of Mnemosyne,
mother full of memories
of the only days in the day.
So close to our house
front-door
in Monster Street,
we keep step
with the Thames flowing by.
In Bishop's Park a Spanish
London plane-tree
made us think of the springs
from which rises the British past

y al cauce de su proceder cedimos
y de este afluente a afluentes
más antes y distantes
de Londres dentro entrados
hacia Coln, Isis, Leach,
por corrientes que arrancan
de Cotswold Hills.
A Londres no entraremos
ni ya nunca de Londres
lograremos salir.
Como si un *paradosso paradisso*
perdido hallado fuera al perseguir
un principio final,
en los Cotswolds entramos
de Londres por la villa
de Bibury (…).
En Hampstead la visión
fue como este graznar sobrevenido
de la cordura al rapto,
del olvido al acuerdo:
el sueño en realidad
de una vigilia en sueños.
La pregunta de Keats no era un dilema.
Seguíamos dormidos y despiertos
el día de los días por venir
ya venido viniendo.
El día que aparenta,
a quien aquí no entra
mientras se adentra
de Londres fuera, ir
a otra tierra cualquiera,
venido sin dejar
de venir: pasajero,
ni anterior ni postrero,
pasaje *advenidero*
en que la flor
dio canto al ruiseñor
y a la rosa color
el canto y cuerpo

tributary of the Rhine,
and we yielded to the channel of its course,
and from this tributary and tributaries
earlier and further away
entered from within London
to Coln, Isis, Leach,
on currents with their source
in the Cotswold Hills.
We won't enter London
nor will we ever succeed
in leaving London.
As if a paradoxical paradise
lost were to be found by seeking
a final beginning,
from London we enter
the Cotswold through the town
of Bibury (...).
In Hampstead the vision
was like the croak coming
from sense to ecstasy,
from forgetting to remembrance:
the real dream
of waking sleep.
Keats's question was not a dilemma.
We were still awake asleep
in the day of days to come,
already here and dawning.
The day appearing,
to whoever doesn't enter
here while entering
out of London, going
to any other country,
here while still
arriving: neither
an early or late passenger,
a passage of becoming
in which the flower
gave the nightingale its song
and colour to the rose

al día el dios
que roza y goza
la rosa el ruiseñor
el ruiseñor la rosa.

song and body
to the day the god
caressing delighting in
the rose the nightingale
the nightingale the rose.

ANTONIO RIVERO TARAVILLO
(Melilla, 1963)

WATERSTONES, PICCADILLY

Las luces mortecinas, como el duelo
por este mundo que desaparece.
Adán sin Eva, soy
el único hombre aquí
—no primero sino último—
esta noche de otoño
en el paraíso de los libros.
Adán sin Eva pero en árabe y hebreo,
sus caracteres reflejados
con refracción disléxica.
Nada
      podrá salvarlos.
Ave
     a los que van a morir
en este edén
en que la enroscada serpiente
es la mondadura de la manzana,
y el árbol del bien y del mal
esta madera negra, los estantes.
Entre susurros las letras
me sisean enseñando los lomos,
los maquillados títulos.
Las contemplo como el erotómano o pornógrafo
que pasa más tiempo en las librerías que leyendo,
más acariciando la posibilidad de acariciar
que acariciando o siendo acariciado.
Tanteo en la tinta como en una noche
llena de agujeros blancos.
El lenguaje oral desparece
en esta catedral del lenguaje escrito,
una capilla ínfima adosada a la gran nave del mundo.
El respirar monocorde de los escasos focos
trae a la velocidad del sonido
la luz de un universo que me asfixia.

ANTONIO RIVERO TARAVILLO

WATERSTONES, PICCADILLY

The dimming lights, like mourning
for this vanishing world.
Eveless Adam, I am
the only man here –
not the first man but the last –
this Autumn night
in the paradise of books.
Eveless Adam but in Arabic and in Hebrew,
their characters reflected
in dyslexic refraction.
Nothing
        could save them.
Hail
     to those who will die
in this Eden
in which the coiled serpent
is the apple peel,
and the tree of good and evil
this black wood, the shelves.
Whispering letters
hiss at me displaying the backs,
the gilt titles.
I gaze at them like the erotomaniac or pornographer
who spends more time in bookshops than reading books,
more time caressing the possibility of caressing
than caressing or being caressed.
I grope around in the ink as in a night
full of white holes.
The spoken language vanishes
in this cathedral of the written,
a tiny chapel attached to the great ship of the world.
The monotonous breathing of the few spotlights
brings at the speed of sound
the light of a universe stifling me.

Pero si no hay oídos ni ojos no hay lengua,
y, mudos, no abiertos, los libros
permanecen vírgenes, plenos de una vida
que en sí misma se agota.
Ahora, en la bajamar del papel
veo luces lejanas en la calle
tras las páginas de cristal.
¿Son barcos que vendrán a rescatarme?
Viernes por la noche, los buques
siguen su curso de derecha a izquierda,
de izquierda a derecha, confundiendo
escrituras y lenguas,
los idiomas del libro.
Diluvia sobre Londres.
En esta arca
hay ejemplares de todas las especies,
parejas de cubiertas y contracubiertas
que llevan inscrito el código genético
de su procreación.
Vértigo, me mareo.
Los renglones se tuercen, la vista
se hermana con el fulgor tan tenue,
Abel que Caín asesina
en el desierto.
¿Hubo pecado? Y si lo hubo, ¿cuál fue?
¿Fue original, o un plagio, un eco,
una traidora traducción?
Como hojas secas mojadas,
la moqueta amortigua la Caída.

But if there are no ears or eyes there is no tongue,
and, mute, unopened, the books
remain virgin, full of a life
dying within itself.
Now, as paper ebbs away
I see distant lights in the street
behind the glass pages.
Are they ships come to rescue me?
On Friday night, boats
follow their courses from right to left,
from left to right, in a confusion
of writings and languages,
book languages.
Rain pours down on London.
In this ark there are editions of all species,
pairs of covers and back covers
with the genetic code of their procreation
inscribed on them.
Vertigo, I'm dizzy.
The lines become deformed, sight
twins with the so tenuous glow,
Abel being killed by Cain
in the desert.
Was there sin? And if there was, what was it?
Was it original, or a plagiarism, an echo,
a treacherous translation?
Like dry damp leaves,
the carpet cushions the Fall.

BALBINA PRIOR
(Villaviciosa de Córdoba, Córdoba, 1964)

BARCO LATINO SOBRE EL TÁMESIS

¿Qué habría yo de buscar en este barco,
en medio de tanto cuerpo de salsa encendido,
desesperado en un país hostil a la cumbia,
que nunca baila con el tercer mundo y, cerrados sus *pubs*
borrachos, ninguna campana para nadie suena?

Londres, como si nada, flota sobre el Támesis,
inmune al pesticida derramado por todas las razas,
pero es una patera con inmigrantes sin dirección ni puerto,
como hinchado pez ilegal muerto sobre las aguas,
como petrolero a punto de vertido,
reventados ya sus tanques y a la deriva.

Desde siempre sin pasaporte como Joseph Conrad,
nada busco en esta inasible oscuridad,
nos vemos siempre obligados a avistar puerto
y, resabiados, acudimos a cualquier lengua,
cualquier alma, cualquier sexo para no estar solos.
Todos los indocumentados hemos encontrado siempre hostal
en la piel bordada del traficante, en los ásperos parques urbanos,
en la doble jornada en restaurantes griegos como Spiro,
incluso en los ojos dorados del sajón y su xenofobia,
abuso vetusto y perfumado de poder egregio.

BALBINA PRIOR

LATIN BOAT ON THE THAMES

What should I hope for on this boat,
surrounded by so many burning salsa bodies,
desperate in a land that hates the Cumbia rhythm,
that never dances with the third world, and when its drunken
pubs are closed no bell rings for anyone?

London, oblivious, floats on the Thames,
immune to the pesticide spilt by every race,
but it's a refugee-boat of harbourless homeless immigrants,
like an illicit blown dead fish on the waters,
like a petrol-tanker about to shed its load,
its tanks already holed, adrift.

Passport-less since birth like Joseph Conrad
I hope for nothing in this heart of darkness,
always we must look for harbour,
hardened we turn to any tongue,
or soul, or sex, so not to be alone.
All of us who have no documents always find hostel
in the embroidered skin of the trafficker, in the rough urban park,
in double shifts at Greek restaurants like Spiro's,
even in the golden eyes of the Saxon and his xenophobia,
the age-old perfumed abuse of haughty power.

JAVIER SÁNCHEZ MENÉNDEZ
(Puerto Real, Cádiz, 1964)

POR EL CENTRO DEL PARQUE

Una duna se mueve como lo hace un verso, sin premeditación. Va dejando que el aire le otorgue esa reserva, sin poder desvelar las contraseñas. Suele ocurrir de noche.

Siempre es mediodía en Kensington Park. Mientras el mundo gira y los ángeles aman, hay una luz que viene y nos convence a todos. Es la luz del misterio, es la propia verdad que nos lleva hasta el sitio, al lugar de la duna. Espacio transparente donde los hombres leen y se crea la poesía. Y en ese instante mismo, tenemos diez minutos para hacernos momentos. Hay silencio. Una mujer pasea en bicicleta y se observa la vida a cámara muy lenta. La sangre de los cuerpos fluye con armonía, se respira diciendo que gozamos de esencia, de la justa verdad, de una sobria expresión sin resultado exacto.

Siempre es mediodía en Kensington Park. No me aparto del centro para seguir tan vivo. Sentado en ese banco te esperaré sonriendo, mientras duren los tiempos podré amarte desnudo, sin nada entre las manos más que un libro de Parra y una rosa amarilla que en Londres he buscado.

Siempre es mediodía en Kensington Park. Llueve un secreto que no desvela nadie y la duna se mueve. La duna es la poesía. Un corazón de arena que el viento determina. Y entre todos los versos, hay una luz helada, la ignición de la palabra siempre en la cultura. El amor de nosotros, los mismos.

JAVIER SÁNCHEZ MENÉNDEZ

IN THE MIDDLE OF THE PARK

A dune is shifting as a verse does, spontaneously. It lets the wind afford one this store, keeping the passwords secret. This usually happens at night.

It's always midday in Kensington Gardens. As the world turns and the angels adore, a light comes and persuades us all. It's the light of mystery, it's truth itself that brings us here, to the dune place. A transparent space where men read and poetry is created. And in that very moment, we have ten minutes to become moments. It's quiet. A woman cycles past and observes life in very slow motion. Blood flows harmoniously in the bodies, one breathes saying that we are enjoying the essential, absolute truth, a sober expression with no particular result.

It's always midday in Kensington Gardens. I don't leave the middle so I can go on being so alive. I'll wait for you sitting on a bench smiling, while the ages last I'll be able to love you naked, with nothing in my hands but a book by Parra and a yellow rose I found in London.

It's always midday in Kensington Gardens. It rains a secret no-one gives away and the dune shifts. The dune is poetry. A heart of sand the wind decides. And in all the verses, there's a frozen light, the firing-up of the word always in culture. Our love, our very own.

MELCHOR LÓPEZ
(Tenerife, 1965)

ALBA PRIMERA

Amanece aquí, en Green Lanes. Amanece en los parques helados de esta tierra. Y más allá, al mismo tiempo, en las arenas negras de las islas amanece.

La mañana abre ya su cola como un ave en un claro sorprendida. Cantan ahora los coros tempranos de los ángeles por las liras pulsadas del aire. Huyen lejos, escapan en su vuelo, todos los pájaros perdidos en las frondas de nuestro mismo sueño. Una mano invisible aparta las sombras y con su palma abierta del primer rayo nos protege.

Amanece, amiga, en las nieves perpetuas del sur, en las lavas imposibles del norte, en la mano que también aparta de tu frente tu pelo. Amanece, aquí, en Green Lanes, amanece de luces desveladas el alba entera. Despierta entonces, amiga, despierta que amanece. Abre ya tus ojos, ábrelos verdes en mi mirada, ábrelos pronto dentro de los míos, en mis ojos rasgados por los pájaros deslumbrados y deslumbrantes del deseo.

MELCHOR LÓPEZ

FIRST DAWN

Dawn is coming here, in Green Lanes. Dawn is coming in the frozen parks of this country. And beyond, at the same hour, dawn is coming over the black sands of the island.

The morning fans its tail like a bird surprised in a clearing. Now sing the early choirs of angels on the plucked lyres of the air. They flee away, off they fly, all the birds lost in the foliage of our dream. An invisible hand pushes the shadows back and with its open palm shelters us from the first ray of sun.

Dawn is coming, sweetheart, in the perpetual snows of the south, in the impossible lavas of the north, in the hand also pushing back your hair from your forehead. Dawn is coming, here, in Green Lanes, the whole dawn comes in light revealed. Wake then, sweetheart, wake for dawn is coming. Open your eyes, green into my eyes, open them quickly into mine, into my eyes torn by the dazzled and dazzling birds of desire.

ANTONIO ORIHUELA
(Moguer, Huelva, 1965)

SEÑALES EN EL AÑO MAYA DEL FIN DEL MUNDO

Comienzo el año maya del fin del mundo intentando seguir
en el códice Colombino del Museo de América
la historia de 8 Venado, un soberano mixteca que,
ayudado por 10 Viento y 1 Lagarto,
entra en contacto con la diosa 9 Caña,
«Señora de las Puntas de Flecha»,
gracias a la ingesta de ciertas sustancias.

Paso luego al códice Madrid,
que es una especie de calendario adivinatorio,
y de ahí camino hacia la sala de los fetiches
donde me encuentro con que en Ghana
se ha puesto de moda enterrarse en ataúdes
decorados como si fueran móviles
y que en Suecia, aunque tampoco dejan pasar a los ilegales,
al menos les han hecho un museo
donde te puedes encontrar
las escaleras con que intentaron saltar la valla de Ceuta.

La siguiente vitrina contiene el espejo negro
con el que el dios Tezcatlipoca
veía todas las cosas y todos los lugares,

—robados por Cortés los dos ejemplares que se conocen,
pasaron a engrosar la colección de Felipe II en El Escorial—

así que acerco mis ojos a su humeante superficie de obsidiana
y sale de ella una cartera que dice London *in your pocket*
con una tarjeta azul que, aseguran, basta enseñar
para poder circular por la ciudad durante una semana.

La siguiente vitrina contiene objetos del Museo Británico,
la gran cueva de Alí Babá de los ingleses, que es
cueva menor al lado de las nuestras, y allí:

ANTONIO ORIHUELA

SIGNS IN THE MAYAN YEAR OF THE END OF THE WORLD

I begin the Mayan year of the end of the world trying to follow,
in the Museo de América's codex Columbino,
the story of 8 Venado, a Mixtec King who,
helped by 10 Wind and 1 Lizard,
comes into contact with the goddess 9 Sugarcane,
'Lady of the Arrowheads',
thanks to the ingestion of certain substances.

Then I move to the Madrid codex,
which is a kind of prophetic calendar,
and from there I go to the fetish room
where I discover that in Ghana
it's become fashionable to be buried in coffins
painted to look like mobile phones
and that in Sweden, although they don't let illegals in either,
at least they've made them a gallery
where you can find
the ladders they tried to get over the Ceuta fence on.

The next case contains the black mirror
in which the god Tezcatlipoca
saw all things and all places

(stolen by Cortés, the two known examples
went on to swell Philip II's collection in the Escorial)

so I move close to peer at the smouldering obsidian surface
and a brochure comes out of it reading *London in your pocket*
with a blue card which you only need to show, they state,
to be able to go anywhere in London for one week.

The next case contains artefacts from the British Museum,
The great Ali Baba's cave of the English, which is
only an minor cave compared to ours, and in it are:

La ola de Hokusai, un extraño grabado de Durero,
un mapa para llegar al corazón de la Meca,
un cuenco micénico adornado con figuritas,
una crátera griega, una invitación a la ceremonia del té,
un sextante árabe con brújula,
un grabado que anuncia la celebración del año del Dragón
y otro mapa que dice que la vida es
dar vueltas alrededor de la casa de Dios.

Más allá, un faraón al que prometieron la inmortalidad
sufre el infierno de ser molestado por varios miles de turistas al día
y en un pasillo otro reposa suavemente su blanca mano
en la de su esposa para poder soportar todo aquello.

La tumba real de Ur, lienzos del palacio de Nimrud y Nínive
decorados con grifos y figuras fantásticas,
la peineta de oro y flores que a mí me hubiera gustado
que lucieras en el día de tu boda,
dragones, samuráis, la piedra Rosetta
mirada con una atención como si los que están delante de ella
fueran todos expertos traductores del demótico al griego antiguo,
los leones asirios y las esculturas del Partenón
que parecen de mantequilla.

Dame un beso que no parta en dos el meridiano de Greenwich,
te digo.

Llévame de la mano hasta el teatro de El Globo
donde se representaron hace siglos las obras de Shakespeare
y a las putas se las llamaba actrices,
o hasta el Golden Hinde, el barco en el que el pirata Drake
dio la vuelta al mundo persiguiendo galeones de oro español,
y al destructor Belfast que está anclado un poco más allá
para que nadie olvide que este es aún un país pirata y guerrero.

I like to be surrounded by pretty things,
leo en una camiseta.

En la otra orilla, unos turistas observan el cambio de guardia,
la cosa resulta tan aburrida que todos prefieren putear un rato

Hokusai's wave, a strange Dürer engraving,
a map to the heart of Mecca,
a Mycenaean bowl adorned with figurines,
a Grecian urn, an invitation to a tea ceremony,
an Arab sextant with compass,
an engraving announcing The Year of the Dragon,
and another map that says that life
revolves around the house of God.

Further on, a pharaoh who was promised immortality
suffers the hell of being pestered by several thousand tourists a day
and in a corridor another one softly reposes his white hand
on his wife's so as to be able to endure it all.

The royal tomb of Ur, canvases from the palace of Nimrod and Nineveh
decorated with gryphons and fantastic figures,
the comb of gold and flowers I'd have liked you
to wear on your wedding day,
dragons, samurai, the Rosetta Stone
intently gazed at as if those in front of it
were all expert translators from the demotic into Ancient Greek,
Assyrian lions, and sculptures from the Parthenon
that look like they're made of butter.

Give me a kiss that doesn't split the Greenwich Meridian in two,
I say to you.

Take me by the hand to the Globe Theatre
where centuries ago Shakespeare's plays were staged
and the whores were called actresses,
or to the Golden Hind, the boat in which the pirate Drake
sailed around the world pursuing galleons filled with Spanish gold,
and to the destroyer H.M.S. Belfast a little further along
so no-one will forget this is still a piratical and warlike country.

I like to be surrounded by pretty things,
I read on a t-shirt.

On the other bank, tourists are watching the changing of the guard,
which is so boring that everybody prefers to spend the time sledging

a los inmóviles caballistas que flanquean el edificio,
de nuevo la imagen de los faraones viene a mi cabeza,
el mundo está lleno de sufrimiento
y de Torres de Londres y libros de Dickens.

Strawberry Hill resulta que además de una canción de los Beatles
es un castillo gótico abierto al público en Twickenham
y la Tate una fábrica de ladrillos hacia donde hoy
cabalga la gente buscando picassos.

Solo frente al matrimonio Arnolfini.
Solo frente al retrato de un joven de Basaiti.
Solo frente al san Francisco meditando de Zurbarán.
Solo frente a don Adrián Pulido Pareja de Martínez del Mazo.
Solo frente a la joven que llora de Béraud.
Solo frente a la Asunción de la Virgen de Vicenza.
Solo ante Susana en el baño de Hayez.
Solo ante la vista de Lowestoft desde el sur de Kerrich.
Solo ante san Jorge y el dragón de Uccello.
Solo frente a una naturaleza muerta de Van de Velde.

Dame un beso que no parta en dos el meridiano de Greenwich,
te digo.

Dame tu mano, llévame al Covent Garden
entre las flores y las verduras de jabón,
llévame al bullicio de sus bares,
al tumulto ordenado de la sangre, sí;
llévame antes de que muera el poeta
entre las flores y las frutas que solo existen en su mente,
antes de que él descubra que la muerte
es irse a vivir al Covent Garden,
desaparecer, como Harry Potter,
en el andén 9 y 3/4 de la estación de King's Cross
o camino de la casa de Sherlock Holmes
en la estación de metro de Baker Street.

Llévame, llévame a la siguiente sala,
a aquella vitrina verde que promete un paseo por Regent's Park

the motionless cavalrymen who flank the building,
once more the image of the pharaohs comes in to my head,
the world is full of suffering
and Towers of London and Dickens novels.

As well as being a Beatles' song, Strawberry Hill
is a Gothic castle in Twickenham open to the public
and the Tate is a brick power-station crowds flock to
nowadays looking for Picassos.

Alone before the Arnolfini Wedding.
Alone before Basaiti's Portrait of a Young Man.
Alone before Zurbarán's Saint Francis in Meditation.
Alone before Martínez del Mazo's Don Adrián Pulido Pareja.
Alone before Béraud's young girl weeping.
Alone before Vicenza's Assumption of the Virgin.
Alone before Hayez's Susanna al Bagno.
Alone before Kerrich's Distant View of Lowestoft from the South.
Alone before Uccello's Saint George and the Dragon.
Alone before a still life by Van de Velde.

Give me a kiss that doesn't split the Greenwich Meridian in two,
I say to you.

Give me your hand, take me to Covent Garden
among the flowers and vegetables made of soap,
take me to the hubbub of its bars,
to the blood's orderly seething, yes;
take me there before the poet dies
amid the flowers and fruits that only exist in his mind,
before he discovers that death
is going off to live in Covent Garden,
vanishing like Harry Potter,
on platform 9 and three-quarters in Kings Cross station
or on the way to Sherlock Holmes's house
in Baker Street underground.

Take me, take me into the next room,
to that green display case that promises a stroll through Regent's Park

desde la casa de Virginia Woolf hasta el mercado de Camden Town,
donde se levantó hace años una modesta placa
en memoria de Felicia Browne, la escultora inglesa
convertida en miliciana
que escribió a finales de julio de 1936

«Dices que estoy huyendo y eludiendo algo al no pintar o esculpir.
Si no hay nada que pintar o esculpir no puedo hacerlo…
Si la pintura o la escultura fueran para mí más valiosas
o urgentes que el terremoto de la revolución… pintaría o esculpiría»,

pero no buscaría la muerte acribillada por las balas fascistas
en Tardienta, Aragón, el 25 de agosto de 1936,
mientras intentaba ayudar a un compañero herido.

THIS PLAQUE COMMEMORATES THE VOLUNTEERS WHO SET OFF FROM THIS BOROUGH TO FIGTH IN THE INTERNATIONAL BRIGADES SPAIN, 1936-1939, AND ALSO THOSE CITIZENS OF THIS BOROUGH WHO SUPPORTED THE SPANISH REPUBLIC IN ITS FIGHT AGAINST FASCISM. **¡NO PASARÁN!**

Es hermoso leer esto, aunque uno sea consciente
de que hace muchos años
que pasaron, a pesar incluso
de los esfuerzos del alcalde Billy Budd,
que se quiso ir con ellos
y no lo dejaron porque solo tenía 16 años;
de todos modos, algo aún se respira en Camden
que tiene otro aire,
que tal vez también se repite
al salir por Notting Hill camino de Portobello Market
y encontrarse con un mosaico que se llama *Ecos de España*
en honor a los voluntarios locales
y los refugiados españoles.

Todo lo demás es bisutería: Soho, Mayfair, Carnaby Street.

Dame un beso que no parta en dos el meridiano de Greenwich,
te digo.

from Virginia Woolf's house to Camden Town market,
where years ago a modest plaque was put up
in memory of Felicia Browne, the English sculptor
who became a freedom fighter
and wrote at the end of July 1936

'You say I'm running away and evading something by not painting or
    sculpting.
If there's nothing to paint or sculpt I can't do it…
If painting or sculpture were more worthwhile or urgent
to me than the earthquake of revolution… I'd paint or sculpt',

but she hadn't thought to die riddled with fascist bullets
in Tardienta, Aragón, on the 25th of August, 1936,
going to the aid of a wounded fellow fighter.

THIS PLAQUE COMMEMORATES THE VOLUNTEERS WHO SET OFF FROM THIS BOROUGH TO FIGHT IN THE INTERNATIONAL BRIGADES SPAIN, 1936-1939, AND ALSO THOSE CITIZENS OF THIS BOROUGH WHO SUPPORTED THE SPANISH REPUBLIC IN ITS FIGHT AGAINST FASCISM. **NO PASARÁN!**

This is lovely thing to read, although we know
that many years ago
they did vanquish, even despite
the efforts of the mayor Billy Budd,
who wanted to go with them
and they didn't let him because he was only 16;
anyway there is a breath of a different air
in Camden,
and perhaps you also catch it
in Notting Hill on the way to Portobello Road market
when you come across a mosaic called *Echoes of Spain*
in honour of the local volunteers
and the Spanish refugees.

All the rest is bling: Soho, Mayfair, Carnaby Street.

Give me a kiss that doesn't split the Greenwich Meridian in two,
I say to you.

Dame la mano pues ya no puedo volar, esta fue mi última primavera,
visito cosas que no existen, cadáveres maquillados
para soportar el paso del tiempo,
faraones egipcios condenados al más cruel de todos los infiernos,
pero también *teddy boys, mods, hippies, punks*, gente cansada
de buscar la isla que no existe, El Dorado, Las Californias,
el barco pirata, los niños descarriados,
el río que dejó hace tiempo la verde llanura.

¿A qué he venido aquí?
¿A ver al menos aquí los mapas del tesoro junto a los tesoros,
aunque sean los mapas y los tesoros de otros, viajes de otros,
vidas de otros que nunca seré?

No ha pasado el tiempo sobre este espejo negro
utilizado para comunicar con espíritus y ángeles
según reza en la cartela,
que fuera un día regalo de Felipe II a John Dee
y que hoy me devuelve, a imagen del que está
en el Museo de América, mis reflejos en el British,
este espejo donde no he dejado de mirar
durante todo este tiempo,
pues la magia sigue necesitando la complicidad del pensamiento
y por eso mismo es hoy una luz que nadie enciende.

Lleva usted razón, este mundo será destruido
y los niños perdidos no habrán podido hacer nada por evitarlo,
todo quedará en unas lágrimas, un sollozo apagado,
no se preocupe, todo está en orden,

ya me voy, sí,
ya sé que va a cerrar el museo.

Give your hand for I can't fly any more, this springtime was my last,
I visit things that don't exist, touched-up corpses
to while away the time,
Egyptian pharaohs condemned to the cruellest hell,
but also *teddy boys, mods, hippies, punks,* people weary
of seeking the enchanted isle, El Dorado, the Californias,
the pirate ship, the lost boys,
the river that left the green fields behind it long ago.

Why did I come here?
To see at least the treasure maps beside the treasure,
although they are other people's maps and treasures, other people's voyages,
others people's lives that never will be mine?

No time has passed on this black mirror
used to communicate with spirits and angels
as it says on the card,
which one day Philip II gave as a present to John Dee
and which now gives back to me, just like the one
in the Museo de América, my reflections in the British Museum,
this mirror I've been gazing into
all this time,
as magic still needs the collusion of thought
and for that very reason is now a light nobody switches in.

You're right, this world will be destroyed
and the lost boys won't have been able to do anything to prevent it,
it'll end in tears, a whimper,
don't worry, all is in order,

I'm off now, yes,
I know the museum is closing.

JUAN LUIS CALBARRO
(Zamora, 1966)

FULGOR DE MADIBA (DICIEMBRE DE 2013)

En Trafalgar, y frente al otro Nelson,
la enseña de Sudáfrica se muestra
en el medio del asta. Los mensajes
de luto y las coronas se amontonan
sobre el adoquinado. La ciudad
luce en la Union Jack, también, su pésame.
En Westminster, el hombre de metal
se dirige a la gente
como guardando aún sabidurías
por enseñar, palabras desde el bronce.
De todas las efigies de Mandela,
la de Londres, con todo y la polémica
factura de Ian Walters, me parece
la más justa: ocultó, precisamente,
el ademán de triunfo, la prestancia
de estadista, de gloria para el mundo
que lo adornan en otros homenajes.
De frente al Parlamento, esa presunta
sede de la palabra,
un inmóvil Madiba reproduce
lo que siempre hizo bien: abrir los brazos.
Si te pones detrás, pierdes de vista
sus ojos, pero puedes apreciar
el gesto: con su pecho siempre abierto,
os quiere persuadir. Y allá, en el otro
costado de la plaza, en perspectiva,
el palacio del diálogo parece
recibir el abrazo de un gigante.

Ya es de noche. Las flores y las notas
le tapizan los pies asendereados
de prisionero erguido, castigado,
y un rosario de velas modestísimas
matizan con temblor de fuego y sombra

JUAN LUIS CALBARRO

MADIBA IN HIS SPLENDOUR (DECEMBER, 2013)

In Trafalgar Square, and facing the other Nelson,
the South African flag hangs
at half mast. Condolences
and wreaths pile up
on the pavement. The city too
mourns with its Union Jack.
In Westminster, the metal man
addresses the people
as if he still had wisdoms
to impart, words from the bronze.
Of all Mandela's statues,
the London one, despite the controversy
over Ian Walters' work, seems to me
the most accurate: precisely because he didn't show
the triumphal pose, the statesmanship,
the worldly glory
given him in other homages.
Opposite the Houses of Parliament,
where the spoken word holds sway,
a motionless Mandiba does
what he always did best: he opens his arms.
If you stand behind him, you can't see
his eyes, but you can appreciate
his stance: with his chest bared
he wants to persuade. And over there, on the other
side of the square, in perspective,
the palace of debate seems
to be held in the arms of a giant.

Night has fallen. Flowers and messages
carpet his worn feet, the feet
of an upright, tortured prisoner,
and a rosary of humble candles
flicker, casting light and shade

aquel fulgor del líder.
Mandela se alza allí, cerca de Palmerston,
de Churchill y de Smuts, de Gandhi y Lincoln,
en el mismo lugar en que en los años
sesenta le dijera a Oliver Tambo,
de visita en el Londres imperial:
«Un día deberían elevar
una estatua de un negro en este parque».
Y los elogios póstumos, postizos
que hoy pronuncian los líderes mundiales
que escucho por la radio a mí me suenan
a civil sacrilegio.
Solo me representan, hoy, las lágrimas
tristísimas y vírgenes del niño
que enciende su candil junto a la basa
mientras mira el fulgor. Mientras se miran.

over the leader's splendour.
Mandela stands here, near Palmerston,
Churchill and Smuts, Gandhi and Lincoln,
in the very place where in the 1960s,
on a visit to imperial London,
he is said to have said to Oliver Tambo:
'One day they should put up the statue
of a black man in this park'.
And the insincere posthumous praise
from world leaders I hear on the radio
sounds to me like
civil sacrilege.
I'm only represented, today,
by the desolate virginal tears of the child
lighting his candle by the plinth
as he regards the splendour. As they regard one another.

JUAN CARLOS ELIJAS
(Tarragona, 1966)

BUNHILL FIELDS O LA POÉTICA DEL BARRENDERO

> *Independientemente de que no podamos percibir*
> *el universo en su totalidad, la imagen es capaz de*
> *expresar esa totalidad.*
> ANDREI TARKOVSKI

I

Ahora, que quizás no sea ahora,
sentado en el banco de la lechuza,
descansa el pulcro barrendero:
la calma verde de las medicinas.

Vivir ahora en la proximidad
del dios de las escobas y los serones,
un silencio incontestable preserva
el advenimiento de la esencia,
la anunciación de lo contrastable
que acaso se confunda con el dios.

Lo elemental era un horno
para calentarse mientras cocía el pan,
los dioses de la harina y la tahona
bajo una luz familiar y distinguida.

El débil sol bebe las copas
de robles y de tilos
entre graznidos de urracas
y serenidad cuáquera.

II

Así el barrendero con la barbilla
apoyada sobre las manos,
las manos sobre el extremo

JUAN CARLOS ELIJAS

BUNHILL FIELDS OR THE POETRY OF THE ROAD SWEEPER

> *Independently of the fact that we can't perceive the universe as a whole, the image is able to express that whole.*
> ANDREI TARKOVSKY

I

Now, which maybe isn't now,
seated on the bench of the owl,
the neat road sweeper takes his rest:
the green calm of medicines.

Living here in the neighbourhood
of the god of brooms and panniers,
an irrefutable silence preserves
the advent of the essence,
the announcement of the verifiable
which perhaps is mistaken for the god.

The elemental was an oven
to warm oneself by while the bread was baking,
the gods of flour and bakery
beneath a familiar distinguished light.

The weak sun drinks the crowns
of oaks and limes
in a squawking of magpies
and Quaker serenity.

II

Thus the sweeper with his chin
resting on his hands,

cilíndrico y desnudo de la escoba,
mientras recuerda las tardes
de invierno acompañando a su abuelo.

La reflexión rememora el ser.
El pensar trabaja en la construcción
de la tumba del ser
y asimila su categoría,
la expresión de su naturaleza.

Verdad indescifrable,
el pensar no crea la tierra
y tanto ser para ser nada,
epitafio célebre para ser barrido.

III

La indiferencia ante la diferencia
entre las losas y las inscripciones,
ante la elipsis del sol.

Salir del tiempo es ser conciencia,
robinsón aislado entre bocadillos
y cafés que consagran el matrimonio
entre la enjundia y el cansancio.

Y ahí, que quizás no sea ahí,
bajo las hojas caídas de los plátanos,
crotoran las cigüeñas negras
en un infierno de infructuosas escrituras.

Los cadáveres recubiertos de miel,
los vinos de palmera que alimentan
las bocas aún conciencia,
los libros de los muertos recitados
en una letanía ataviada para la salvación
con dos monedas brunas en los ojos.

his hands on the naked
cylindrical tip of his broomstick,
remembering winter afternoons
with his grandfather.

Reflection brings back the person.
Thought toils to build
the tomb of the person,
and absorbs his likeness,
the expression of his nature.

An indecipherable truth,
thought does not create the earth
and so much life to come to nothing,
a famous epitaph to be wiped away.

III

Indifference in the face of the difference
between the gravestones and what is written on them
in the face of the ellipsis of the sun.

To come out of time is to be consciousness,
Robinson castaway among sandwiches
and coffees that consecrate a marriage
between matter and weariness.

And there, which maybe isn't there,
under the fallen leaves of the plane-trees,
the black storks clatter
in a hell of barren script.

The honey-covered corpses,
the palm wines feeding
mouths still consciousness,
the books of the dead declaimed
in a litany spruced up for salvation
with two brown coins on its eyes.

Yo no he venido aquí
—así el poeta a orillas del Támesis—
para hablar de mi infancia
como un león farmacéutico y felino.

I didn't come here –
as the poet on Thames shore –
to speak of my childhood
like a sly pharmaceutical lion.

SUSANA MEDINA
(Hampshire, 1966)

FRAGMENTO DE MAPA EMOCIONAL

Y cada equis tiempo,
por una razón u otra,
la visita ritual a la colina de Primrose Hill
y, de paso, a Chalcot Square, a la casa donde solían vivir
cuando eran estudiantes
y el tiempo apenas les había rozado.

Y en los últimos años, cuando hay amigos que vienen a Londres
y duermen en su sofá cama tras patearse la ciudad,
una de las noches los llevan a dar una vuelta por los alrededores,
que incluye Abbey Road, y cruzar a zancadas el famoso paso de cebra,
y la visita ritual es el destino del *tour* nocturno.

Y cuando suben por el césped húmedo a la cima de Primrose Hill
les muestran la impresionante vista panorámica de casi 360 grados,
y con el dedo nombran diferentes edificios, y resumen sus historias,
y la silueta de la ciudad va cambiando,
y el *skyline* iluminado va acogiendo más mensajes y luces,
y últimamente ha brotado una serie de grúas de construcción
que en la noche se revisten de luz roja, haciendo resaltar el *boom*
                                                            inmobiliario.

Y ella siempre les lee con una sonrisa la inscripción grabada
en un amplio bordillo curvado de una cita de William Blake:
I have conversed with the spiritual Sun. I saw him on Primrose Hill,
y es un momento mágico.
Y también les cuentan que cerca de aquí, cavaron una pequeña fosa,
y enterraron a su hámster, Orlando,
y que en *La guerra de los mundos*, H. G. Wells eligió esta colina
para el último aterrizaje de los marcianos.
Y en la última visita, apuntan a la Torre BT,
uno de los edificios más emblemáticos,
y añaden unas líneas nuevas a la narrativa:
cuando murió Bowie,
su pantalla electrónica giratoria

SUSANA MEDINA

FRAGMENT OF EMOTIONAL MAP

And every now and then,
for one reason or another,
the ritual visit to Primrose Hill,
and, on the way, Chalcot Square, where they lived
when they were students,
almost untouched by life.

And in recent years, when friends come to London
and sleep on the sofa-bed, after traipsing through the city,
on one of the nights they take them for a spin round the neighbourhood,
including Abbey Road, to cross the famous zebra-crossing in giant strides,
and the ritual visit rounds off the nocturnal tour.

And when they climb the damp grass to the top of Primrose Hill
they show them the impressive almost 360 degree panorama,
and they point out and name the various buildings and explain their history,
and the silhouette of the city keeps changing,
and the illuminated skyline adds to its messages and lights,
and lately a series of cranes has sprung up,
bathed in red light by night, highlighting the housing boom.

And with a smile she always reads them the quotation from Blake
inscribed on a curved wide kerb:
I have conversed with the spiritual sun. I saw him on Primrose Hill,
and it's a magical moment.
And they also tell them that near here, they dug a little hole,
and buried their hamster, Orlando,
and that in *The War of the Worlds,* H. G. Wells chose this hill
for the final landing-place of the Martians.
And in the most recent visit, they point to the BT Tower,
one of the more iconic buildings,
and they add some new lines to the story:
when Bowie died,
its electronic revolving screen

emitió tristísima en letras mayúsculas luminosas blancas:
DESCANSA EN PAZ, DAVID BOWIE.

Y siempre suelen, de paso, mostrarles la casa donde vivieron,
y les cuentan que, al lado, en esta casa de aquí, vivió Silvia Plath.
Y no, en esta casa no fue donde se suicidó:
esta es la casa donde vivió.
Se suicidó en una calle por aquí cerca, Fitzroy Road,
en la casa donde había vivido William Butler Yeats.
Y antes no estaba la placa azul circular de Patrimonio Inglés:
la deben de haber puesto hace poco.
Y enfrente de nuestra casa vivía un capitán de barco
que tenía un Cadillac descapotable y un dálmata
que solía viajar erguido en la parte de atrás.

Y los amigos vuelven a sus respectivos países
llenos de historias, y dentro de esas historias,
están insertas las historias de sus amigos,
que también contienen historias de otros.
Y todo es flujo y todo cambia,
y, por una razón u otra,
cada equis tiempo, la visita ritual.

displayed mournfully in luminous white capitals:
REST IN PEACE, DAVID BOWIE.

And they always show them, in passing, the house where they lived,
and they tell them that, next door, in this house here, Sylvia Plath lived.
And, no, she didn't kill herself there.
She killed herself nearby, in Fitzroy Road,
in the house where William Butler Yeats had once lived.
And the English Heritage round blue plaque wasn't there then:
they must have put it up fairly recently.
And opposite our house lived a ship's captain
who had a Cadillac convertible and a Dalmatian
who always rode sitting up in the back.

And the friends go back to their respective countries
full of stories, and into these stories
are inserted the stories of their friends,
which also have other people's stories in them.
And all is in flux and everything changes,
and, for one reason or another,
every so often, the ritual visit.

DAVID TORRES
(Madrid, 1966)

EL PUENTE

Esta es la puerta. Este es el final.
Aquí el pasillo que conduce a la calle.
Aquí los escalones que descienden al miedo.
Antorchas congeladas sobre las aceras,
Señales en un libro leído y releído.
Nadie pudo cruzar Londres a pie en una noche.
Siempre alguien lo intenta, no obstante:
Un viajero extraviado con un par de maletas,
Un barrendero que empuja los desechos,
Una mujer de zapatos raídos murmurando.
Todo termina aquí. Todo empieza.
Cortejando envoltorios y periódicos viejos
La escoba ha llegado hasta el río.
El barrendero lanza un escupitajo al agua,
Se le ocurre que los diarios atrasados son flores,
Son mariposas que duran solo un día.
Hay palabras que sobreviven siglos, otras
Mueren apenas pronunciadas. El barrendero
Siente sed, piensa una cerveza, hace una bola
Con sus pensamientos, la arroja al suelo.
Hay palabras que mueren antes de pronunciarse,
Hay deseos que ni siquiera afloran.

Como una araña enamorada de su propia tela
La luna escupe baba sobre el puente.
La mujer pálida no sabe para qué sirve el río.
Simplemente se alza sobre sus talones y mira
El reflejo de la luna, blanco sobre negro,
Peniques plateados, cabellos de doncellas.
Oscuras aguas murmuran en lenguajes
Demasiado antiguos para ser descifrados.
Hablan de reinos perdidos, de leyendas
Tan lejanas como el día de ayer o la infancia.
La saliva golpea, se expande en ondas,

DAVID TORRES

THE BRIDGE

This is the door. This is the end.
Here the corridor leading to the street.
Here the steps descending to fear.
Frozen lamps on the pavements.
Signs in a book read and reread.
No-one could cross London on foot in one night.
But someone always tries:
A lost traveller with a couple of suitcases,
A road-sweeper nudging litter forward,
A woman in shabby shoes muttering.
Everything ends here. Everything begins.
Pushing wrappers and old newspapers
The broom has got to the river.
The road-sweeper spits in the water,
It crosses his mind that yesterday's papers are flowers,
Are butterflies who live for one day.
Some words last through the ages, others
Die on the lips. The road-sweeper
Feels thirsty, he thinks of a beer, he rolls up
His thoughts in a ball, he throws it onto the ground.
Some words die before they're spoken aloud.
Some desires don't even make it to the surface.

Like a spider in love with its own web
The moon drools over the bridge.
The pale woman doesn't know what the river is for.
She just stands on her heels and looks at
The moon's reflection, white on black,
Silver pennies, maidenhair.
Dark words murmur in languages
Too ancient to decipher.
They tell of lost kingdoms, legends
As far away as yesterday or childhood.
The saliva hits, spreads out in waves,

La luz de la luna flota en círculos.
La mujer pálida y despeinada se quita un zapato.
Tiene un calcetín roto, pero no siente el frío,
Sino el cansancio de sesenta años goteando uno a uno.
Ahora se ha detenido en mitad del puente,
Mira el cadáver cromado de la luna temblando, temblando.

Todo lo que sucede, sucedió alguna vez.
Todo lo que sucederá, ha sucedido.
No sirve de nada lamentarse, arrepentirse,
Llorar los días muertos de los calendarios,
En los pequeños nichos de los números.
El asesino no lamenta su crimen,
Ni el río sabe cuántos ahogados arrastra.

El viajero que acarrea sudando su equipaje
No llegará a tiempo a la estación.
Cómo encontrar un taxi que lo lleve al pasado:
No Babilonia o Nínive, solo unas horas atrás,
Kensington, un cuarto alquilado en un hotel,
Una mujer que lo acaricia en silencio
Mientras oyen una música que avanza y avanza.
La humedad en la alfombra y el tiempo en las paredes.
Porque ahora mismo, hace un rato, ayer,
Son tan inaccesibles como la infancia,
Como Babilonia, como esa mujer que se va calle abajo,
Como eras geológicas o mascotas muertas.
Y los recuerdos: artesanos ciegos, mancos,
Reconstruyendo estatuas que se han licuado en barro,
Hundiendo los muñones en el lodo del tiempo.

De pie, bajo las luces, el viajero desdeña el frío.
Deja el equipaje en el suelo un instante, se olvida,
Permite que la ciudad lo inunde o lo vacíe,
Que la madrugada se empape de sí misma
Para que los figurantes que la pueblan
Sean por una vez hombres y mujeres.
Esto es la ciudad. Esto es ahora.
El aliento del niño dormido, el aire

The moonlight floats in rings.
The pale dishevelled woman takes off a shoe,
She has a hole in her sock but she doesn't feel the cold,
Only the weariness of 60 years drop by drop.
Now she has stopped in the middle of the bridge
She looks at the chromed cadaver of the moon trembling, trembling.

Everything that happens, has already happened.
Everything that will happen, has happened before.
It's useless to regret, repent,
Mourn the dead days on the calendar,
Numbered in their little boxes,
The murderer does not repent of his crime,
The river doesn't know how many drowned it bears away.

The traveller sweating lugging his cases
Won't make it to the station in time.
How to find a taxi to take him to the past:
Not Babylon or Nineveh, just a few hours back,
Kensington, a rented hotel room,
A woman silently caressing him
As they listen to music playing on and on.
Damp in the carpet and time on the walls.
Because now, a while ago, yesterday
Are out of reach as childhood,
As Babylon, as that woman going away down the street,
As geological eras or dead pets.
And memories: blind artisans, the maimed
Resculpting statues liquefied to mud,
Burying their stumps in the clay of time.

Standing beneath the lamps, the traveller scorns the cold.
He drops his bags on the ground for a moment, his mind wanders,
He lets the city flood or empty him,
Lets the dawn steep in its own substance
So that the extras who people it
For once might be women and men.
This is the city. This is now.
The breath of the sleeping child, the wind

Oliendo a leche, los juguetes desterrados
Del suave naufragio de la cuna.
El portero que cabecea en su caseta
Demasiado somnoliento para encender la radio.
La joven que se masturba a solas en la cama.
El asesino que afila otra vez sus cuchillos.
El barrendero que entra en un bar y pide una cerveza.
Los amantes desesperadamente entrelazados,
Agotados, como si ésta fuera la última vez
O la primera, como el alcohólico que jura
Tomar su último trago, pero nunca
Es el último, sino el primero.
Una música que avanza y avanza.

El amor, el río, la vida, el tiempo
Fluyen en un solo sentido.
Nada ni nadie, ni siquiera Dios, puede
Dar marcha atrás, remover la corriente,
Devolver el semen que se enfría sobre unos muslos tibios
O la sangre secándose sobre unas baldosas.

La mujer sigue detenida en mitad del puente,
Sola, descalza, hablando con el viento.
Ha arrojado un zapato y luego el otro.
Lárgate a casa, hombre, ya es tarde.
El borracho golpea el codo del barrendero
Y le suelta un sermón de madrugada,
Tropezando con las palabras, escupiéndolas.
No se enamore nunca, amigo,
Nunca cierre los ojos en medio de un beso
Porque nunca se sabe cuándo llega el amor
Del mismo modo que no se sabe nunca
Cuándo el sueño nos atrapa. Sí, señor,
Una cabezada, un parpadeo, y estás listo.
Ben, ponme una a mí y otra al caballero.
El camarero que ensaya su paciencia con la barra,
Los amantes que suspiran exhaustos, separados
Por desiertos de carne, por recuerdos y espejos,
La anciana que, sentada ante el tocador,

That smells of milk, the toys banished
From the soft shipwreck of the cradle.
The porter nodding in his little hut
Too sleepy to switch his radio on.
The young woman masturbating, alone in her bed.
The murderer resharpening his knives.
The road-sweeper going into a pub and ordering a beer.
The lovers desperately entwined,
Spent, as if this were the last time,
Or the first, like the drunkard who swears
This drink is my last, but it never is
The last drink, but the first.
A music that plays on and on.

Love, the river, life and time
Flow in one direction.
Nothing and no-one, not even God himself,
Can turn back, reverse the current,
Return the semen cooling on warm thighs
Or the blood drying on the paving-stones.

The woman is still standing in the middle of the bridge,
Alone and barefoot, talking to the wind.
She has thrown off first one shoe, then the other.
Go home, man, before it's too late.
The drunk slaps the road-sweeper's elbow
And preaches him a dawn sermon,
Stumbling over his words, spitting them out.
Never fall in love, my friend.
Never shut your eyes in the middle of a kiss
Because we never know when love is coming
Just as we never know
When sleep takes us. Yes sir,
A nod, a blink and we're gone.
Ben, one for me and one for the gent.
The patient barman,
The spent lovers, sighing, parted
By deserts of flesh, memories and mirrors,
The old woman sitting at her dressing-table

Intenta alisar el pasado, disfrazar sus arrugas,
El asesino que se desnuda a oscuras
En el cuarto de baño y se sumerge
En una bañera llena de sangre tibia,
Juegan el mismo juego.

Aunque el pasado todavía está sucediendo
Nadie puede volver sobre sus pasos.
Ni siquiera el río puede esquivar el puente.
La mujer pálida sigue aferrada a las piedras.
Mira hacia abajo, hacia ese flujo negro, negro:
Ningún hijo podría salir de allí, ninguna cara.
La joven solitaria cuyo orgasmo es tan triste como la luna,
El barrendero que invita a un negro melancólico antes de irse,
El negro que cabecea y ni siquiera da las gracias,
Piensan que bajo cada rostro vive una calavera,
Recuerdan que tras su sonrisa asomarían gusanos,
Si no fuera por el tiempo, marcando los compases,
Dando cuerda a relojes y ciudades.
El borracho sale del bar, tropieza en un callejón,
Cae junto a unos cubos de basura, se echa a llorar
De pronto, sin saber si esas lágrimas son suyas,
Lamentando una vida que no le pertenece
Porque el pasado lo dejó atrás, huérfano
De destinos, otro pez atrapado en las redes
Del viento, el viento, el viento y sus caladeros:

El viajero que ha dejado escapar su tren,
El asesino que desayuna despacio
Sin más remordimientos que la molestia
De tener que fregar el baño antes de ir al trabajo,
El vagabundo que se desgañita a gritos en la calle,
No hay nadie, no hay nadie, no hay nadie, no hay nadie,
Y el negro que murmura, sabes, me gustan
Las tías una pizca gordas, son oráculos,
Documentos indescifrables, fragmentos
De una música que sigue y sigue.

La luz en la ventana, el escritor aficionado
Repasando sus hojas mientras sorbe un café,

Trying to smooth over the past, mask her wrinkles,
The murderer undressing in the dark
In the bathroom and sinking into
A bath of warm blood,
All are playing the same game.

Though the past is still ongoing,
No-one can retrace his steps.
Not even the river can avoid the bridge.
The pale woman doesn't move from the pavement.
She gazes down on the black, black water.
No child could emerge from it, no face.
The lonely young woman, whose orgasm is as sad as the moon,
The road-sweeper who buys a gloomy black a drink, and leaves,
The black who nods and doesn't thank him,
All see the skull beneath the skin,
Remember that worms may slide out of a smile,
If it weren't for time keeping the beat,
Winding up the clocks and the cities.
The drunk leaves the pub, stumbles in an alleyway,
Falls over by the dustbins, bursts into tears
All at once, uncertain if the tears are his,
Mourning a life that isn't his
Because the past outdistanced him, orphan
Of fate, another fish caught in the nets
Of the wind, the wind, the wind, and its fishing-grounds.

The traveller who has let his train leave without him,
The murderer enjoying a leisurely breakfast,
remorseless, but irritated
At having to scrub out the bath before work,
The tramp screaming in the street,
There is nobody, nobody, no-one is there,
And the black muttering, you know, I like
Women with flesh on their bones, all are oracles,
Undecipherable documents, fragments
Of a music that plays on and on.

A light in his window, the eager writer
Revising his work, sipping his coffee,

Leyendo todo lo que la ciudad le regaló una vez
Y que él intentó devolver a la calle,
Siente que las palabras son cera, piedra, arcilla, no amor:
El asesino está más cerca de la verdad de la vida
Cuando exprime una bayeta empapada de sangre.

La música, los amantes se duermen, sueñan juntos,
Pegados, abrazados, pero ninguno puede
Saber qué sueña el otro, nadie puede
Amar del todo a alguien, aunque entregue su vida.
Nadie asegura que el funcionario sonriente
Tras la ventanilla no sea el carnicero
De quien hablan todos los periódicos
Arrastrados por la marea de la tarde. Nadie
Sabe si el borracho caído en el suelo duerme.
Pero la luz llama en todos los tejados.
La mujer pálida termina de cruzar el puente,
Se aleja arrastrando los pies descalzos.
Tampoco el río pudo elegir su camino.
Este es el final. Esta es la puerta.

Reading over all the city gave him once
And what he tried to give back to the streets,
Feels words are wax, stone, clay and never love:
The murderer is closer to the truth of life
Squeezing out a blood-soaked handkerchief.

Music, the lovers fall asleep, they dream together,
Clasped, glued the one to the other, though neither
Knows what the other dreams, no-one can give
Absolute love to anyone, though he surrender his life.
No-one can be confident the smiling clerk
Behind the window is not the butcher
We read about in all the papers
Borne away on the evening tide. No-one
Knows if the drunk on the pavement is asleep
But daylight points on all the roofs.
The pale woman has made it to the other side of the bridge,
And heads off, dragging her bare feet.
Nor can the river choose its course.
This is the end. This is the door.

JORDI DOCE
(Gijón, 1967)

DÍAS DE 1998

A Cristina y Jon

En Thames Walk, las gaviotas saqueaban el fango bajo una luz metálica o subían sin más, girando sobre el puente de Hammersmith como grandes esporas. Venían de muy lejos, con la marea baja y el olor del salitre, y se instalaban entre restos de plástico, charcos de aceite y leños andrajosos, la basura tenaz de los bajíos. *Nada era nuestro entonces, solo aquellas conversaciones, la fresca letanía de agravios y cansancios, el peso muerto de la expectativa caminando sin prisa a nuestro lado.* Allí, sobre la celda del tiempo compartido, la brisa del Atlántico mordía las maderas y el cemento, velaba la otra orilla donde a veces, a media tarde, el sol mediocre de noviembre hacía relumbrar los descampados. *Se adensaba en los muros la penumbra y nosotros hablábamos, hablábamos, llevados de la mano de la urgencia, escrutando unas aguas que nada duplicaban.*

Era el Londres de Blake, con sus calles censadas y sus fraguas satánicas, la niebla parda de la irrealidad, el río abandonado por sus ninfas, la fábrica de gas, el cielo donde torres de ladrillo ondeaban su fuego seco. *Ahora sé que el deseo de ser oscurecía el ser, que la sangre no fluye a voluntad.* Una vez, en la orilla, vimos brillar la cola de una rata. Una serpiente negra, un látigo de insidia. Regresaba a su hogar, como nosotros, bajo la luz de las farolas, soldado en su trinchera de despojos. *Hurtarnos al presente era una forma de inventar otro nuevo, de alzar con negaciones la quimera del sí.* Nos intrigó su piel, la blandura del lomo, ese moverse a tientas junto al muro como queriendo no ser vista. *El aire espeso, pensativo, se engastaba en la piel como una especia, borrando manchas y cicatrices, tomando posesión de su dominio.* La vimos husmear, perderse entre las matas con suavidad grasienta hasta que sonó un grito, de pronto, y despertamos. *Obedientes al frío, acogimos su aliento hasta formar con él un rostro nuevo, hecho de espera y esperanza, y otra vez fuimos vulnerables.*

2004, 2018

JORDI DOCE

DAYS OF 1998

For Cristina and Jon

On Thames Walk, the gulls plundered the mud in the metallic light or swooped up abruptly, circling over Hammersmith Bridge like large spores. They came from a great distance, with the low tide and the saltpetre smell, and they landed among bits of plastic, pools of oil and rotten wood, the stubborn flotsam of the shallows. *Nothing was ours then, only those conversations, the fresh litany of grievances and weariness, the dead weight of expectation strolling beside us.* There, above the prison of shared time, the Atlantic breeze bit into the wood and concrete, veiled the other bank, where sometimes, halfway through the afternoon, the measly November sun gave a glow to the wastelands. *The half-light congealed on the walls and we talked and talked, compulsively, gazing into waters which gave nothing back.*

It was Blake's London, with its chartered streets and its satanic mills, the brown fog of unreality, the river abandoned by its nymphs, the gas-holders, the sky where brick towers shimmered their dry fire. *Now I know that the yearning to be darkened being, that the blood doesn't flow at will.* Once, on the riverbank, we saw a rat's tail lit up. A black serpent, a whiplash of malice. It was returning to its hearth, like us, in the lamplight, a soldier in its trench of spoil. *Stealing away from the present was a way of inventing a different one, of raising through negation the chimera of acceptance.* We were intrigued by its skin, its soft back, its creeping by the wall as if it didn't want to be seen. *The thick, pensive air settled on its skin like a spice, wiping stains and scars away, taking possession of its demesne.* We saw it catching a scent, vanishing into the undergrowth with its greasy softness, till a scream rang out, and we awoke. *Obeying the cold, we welcomed its breath until we had made from it a new face, made of patience and hope, and we were vulnerable once more.*

2004, 2018

ANXO CARRACEDO
(La Coruña, 1970)

[EN AQUELLA ÉPOCA...]

   Londres, 1993

En aquella época
yo tenía la barba negra
y los ojos no me dejaban
ver la barba

en aquella época
mis vecinas tenían las tetas tristes
como platos de polenta tibia
y yo caminaba
con cuchillos en los ojos

en aquella época
los chaperos del parque
me saludaban con la punta de los dedos
y la mujer del quiosco
me daba noticias

   la del notario cocainómano
   y la del trapecista ciego

que no cabían en las secciones
de sucesos

en aquella época
yo salía a la calle sin palomas
y en tus manos se hacía febrero
mientras las maletas del I.R.A.
pedían silencio

  would you please?

a las roncas guitarras
en el metro

ANXO CARRACEDO

[BACK THEN...]

London, 1993

Back then
my beard was black
and my eyes wouldn't let me
look at my beard

back then
my neighbours had tits as depressing
as cooling polenta
and I went about
with knives in my eyes

back then
the gay guys in the park
waved their fingertips at me
and the woman in the kiosk
fed me stories

      the one about the cokehead lawyer
      and the one about the blind trapeze-artist

that didn't appear
in the newspapers

back then
I went out doveless
and it was February in your hands
while the I.R.A. suitcases
asked for silence

      would you please?

from the hoarse guitars
on the underground

en aquella época
yo huía de las palomas
y preguntaba
a las azules manos del invierno
cuántas veces ha de decir un hombre
    lo siento
antes de saber
que camina
con cuchillos en los ojos

en aquella época

        la del notario cocainómano
        las palomas miserables
        y el trapecista ciego

llevabas las respuestas
en el pelo.

back then
I ran away from doves
and asked
winter's blue hands
how many times must a man say
    I'm sorry
before he realizes
he's going about
with knives in his eyes

back then, at the time of

        the cokehead lawyer
        the mournful doves
        and the blind trapeze-artist

you wore the answers
in your hair.

FRANCISCO LEÓN
(Tenerife, 1970)

[RENACE LA MAÑANA...]

Renace la mañana en Brookhill Road. Se estremecen las hojas de los árboles muertos, la escarcha de las ramas podridas. Renace la mañana y el frío hondo de la tierra macilenta abandona furtivo las esquinas de la noche. La brisa se deshace lentamente como el cuerpo de una muerta que vagara sus últimos instantes por las calles de este Woolwich Arsenal al que he venido. Renace la mañana, sí, revive la luz que entrega a cada cosa los pulsos nuevos de la sangre por los torrentes del sueño. Revive el canto de las cornejas en los parques mojados, el trasiego inquieto de las ardillas. Oigo a Mohamed que comienza en el cuarto contiguo sus plegarias, y al joven Nick, chino-americano con sus discos, y al oscuro y sucio Tomás el judío, y todos, redimidos, renacen al alba con la luz primera de este mundo y sus ciclos cansados y repetidos, y así el alba en la niebla, esta mañana en que soy uno más de estos hombres, se llena de dioses distintos y de ángeles vestidos con extrañas armaduras y túnicas y saris y pieles de tigre, y una luz divina y dulce envuelve el sueño de los que aún duermen y esperan despertar mañana más allá de los mares y los desiertos y las montañas, en la transparencia irreal de un Edén en la tierra.

FRANCISCO LEÓN

[NEW MORNING...]

New morning in Brockhill Road. The leaves on dead trees, the frost on rotten branches, shudder. New morning and the bone cold of the emaciated land steals away from the corners of night. The breeze slowly dissolves like the corpse of a woman who spent her last moments wandering the streets of Woolwich Arsenal where I am now. New morning, yes, light revives giving to each thing a new pulse of blood through the torrents of dream. The cawing of crows in the sodden parks revives, and the restless to and fro of squirrels. I hear Mohammed in the next room beginning his prayers, and Nick, a Chinese American playing his records, and dark and scruffy Jewish Thomas, and all, redeemed, in the new dawn in the first light of this world and its tired repetitive cycles, and so this foggy dawn, this morning where I am one more mortal, fills with strange gods and angels wearing strange armour and tunics and saris and tiger skins, and a soft and divine light envelops the dreams of those still asleep who wish to wake to a morning beyond the seas and deserts and mountains, in the unreal transparency of an earthly Eden.

JULIO MAS ALCARAZ
(Madrid, 1970)

ST. PAUL

A Dhia Chandraratna

Al amanecer, el rocío cubría las lonas impermeables de las tiendas de campaña de marca e incluso había borrado parte de los carteles utópicos pintados sobre cartones de Harrods.

En la fuente de la reina Anne todavía flotaba el zapato de piel de caballo de un niño de Eton y se hundía el tubo de rímel con el que ella dibujaba grafitis.

Ella, a la que encontré con un diente roto, una maceta con geranios rojos y restos de sangre seca en la comisura de sus labios.

Le dolía la boca pero nos besamos.

*

Había olvidado qué era un recuerdo y cómo se enfrenta a sí mismo ante el espejo de unos adoquines mojados por la lluvia.

Todo esto ocurrió al lado del hombre que leía un libro de Gramsci sosteniéndolo con una sola mano: el lector cigüeña.

Occupy London lo llamaron, y ocupamos los alrededores de una iglesia ostentosa y mencionamos la palabra revolución.

Si Jesús volviera y viera esto, decían algunos. Como si pudiese. Como si *St. Paul* no se escurriera por esas escaleras que tienen algo de esquejes de un edificio superior inexistente. Como si pudiéramos tomar en serio un templo que acoge el cuerpo de Henry Fuseli, el mismo que rechazó la oferta divina de Mary Wolfstonecraft para formar un trío.

Ocupar

JULIO MAS ALCARAZ

ST. PAUL

For Dhia Chandraratna

Dawn, and the dew covered the waterproof tarps of the swanky tents and had even washed away part of the utopian slogans painted on Harrods cardboard.

In the Queen Anne fountain the horsehide shoe of an Etonian was still afloat and the tube of mascara that she used to write graffiti was sinking.

She, who I met with a broken tooth, a pot of red geraniums and dried blood on the corner of her lips.

Her mouth hurt but we kissed.

*

I had forgotten what a memory was and how it comes face to face with itself in the mirror of rain-drenched cobbles.

All this happened beside a man reading a book by Gramsci holding it aloft in one hand: the stork reader.

Occupy London they called it and we occupied the outside of an overweening church and uttered the word revolution.

If only Jesus came back and saw this, some said. As if he could. As if *St. Paul* weren't melting down these steps which look like a transplant from some non-existent grander building. As if we could take seriously a church that houses the remains of Henry Fuseli, who turned down Mary Wollstonecraft's divine proposal of a threesome.

Occupy

Londres. Donde la Reina aparta la cortina con los dedos para observar las erecciones de los Guardias de Gales cuando se ponen firmes.
Londres. Donde Jimi Hendrix se ahoga en su propio vómito negro mientras Monika practica patinaje artístico en el pasillo.
Londres. Donde un traficante de marfil amante del electrolatino compra la casa de Amy Winehouse.
Maldita ciudad donde los comunistas guardan las hojas que caen sobre la tumba de Karl Marx para que su nostalgia dure al menos hasta la primavera, porque en verano viajan a sus mansiones de Ibiza.
Donde Yoko Ono manda que su chófer acelere cada vez que atraviesa el paso de cebra de Abbey Road.
Donde un magnate ruso juega con la colección de figuritas que adquirió a la fundación Freud y duda entre comprarse otro equipo de fútbol o cambiar de sitio la jirafa disecada.
Donde T. S. Eliot, empleado de banco en Lloyds, trabaja durante años en un sótano tan triste que se hace anglocatólico.
Donde William Blake, esa mancha de color que volaba para no pisar las alfombras de tigre, es enterrado al lado de jaulas de petirrojos sin que ni siquiera su nombre se muestre en la lápida.
Donde esperamos en vano que la rueda del *London Eye* se marche rodando en dirección al mar y se use como faro o pieza artística con turistas atrapados.

No. *St. Paul* es otra cosa: antidisturbios que conocen los nombres de los componentes de *Sex Pistols* de mi camiseta, una cúpula asentada como un gigantesco Buda que esconde su cabeza de la lluvia y cuatro colores incompletos por debajo de una mano.

St. Paul es, por siempre, donde quedan los banqueros de la *City* con sus camellos y, en la espera, se masturban al contemplar los techos cubiertos con pan de oro y llaman a los monaguillos a los rincones para meterles billetes de 50 libras en la ropa interior.

*

Sonaron los helicópteros, vino la policía, nos dispersaron y nunca más te volví a ver.

London. Where the Queen draws back the curtain to observe the erections
    of the Welsh Guards when they stand at attention.
London. Where Jim Hendrix drowns in his own black vomit
    while Monika figure skates down the corridor.
London. Where an ivory trader electrolatino aficionado buys
    Amy Winehouse's house.
Accursed city where communists collect the leaves from Karl Marx's grave
    so that their nostalgia will last till the spring at least,
    because in summer they're off to their villas in Ibiza.
Where Yoko Ono orders her chauffeur to hit the accelerator every time
    she drives over the Abbey Road zebra-crossing.
Where a Russian magnate plays with the collection of figurines he acquired
    from the Freud Foundation and dithers between buying another
    football team or moving his stuffed giraffe.
Where T. S. Eliot, a clerk at Lloyds Bank, works for years in a basement
    so depressing he becomes Anglo-Catholic.
Where William Blake, that splash of colour who took to the air so as not
    to tread on tiger-skin rugs, is buried next to caged robins
    in an unmarked grave.
Where we wait in vain for the *London Eye* to roll off
    seawards and serve as a lighthouse or as an installation
    with tourists trapped inside it.

No, *St. Paul* is something else: riot police who know the names
    of the *Sex Pistols* on my t-shirt, a dome sitting
    like a gigantic Buddha covering his head against
    the rain with four unfinished colours under one hand.

St. Paul eternally is where the City bankers rendezvous with their
    drug dealers and, while they wait, wank as they gaze at the gold-
    leaf roofs and summon altar-boys into corners
    to stuff £50 notes in their underpants.

*

The helicopters whirred, the police arrived, they dispersed us and
I never saw you again.

En solo veinticuatro horas nos habíamos prometido besos sin sangre, cantar juntos por el mundo y apretar la existencia hasta rompernos las manos en una vida.

Debería lamentar lo que podríamos haber sido, pero Bowie ha muerto, su cuerpo no yace en el altar mayor y las memorias arden de esa manera extraña en la que se retuercen las diapositivas al acercarlas a una llama.

Si algún día, de forma milagrosa, traducen este poema y te reconoces en él, no llames a la editorial a buscarme. Ya no tendremos fuerza ni sueños para cantar, y quién quiere besarse sin heridas.

Qué mejor que un recuerdo, como cuando los árboles tenían invierno y aves, e incluso un futuro afuera de Kew Gardens.

In just twenty-four hours we had promised each other kisses with no
blood, to sing in harmony for the world, and to squeeze existence till we
broke our hands, in one life.

I should mourn what we could have been but Bowie is dead, his body
is not lying on the high altar and the memories are burning
in the strange way negatives do when you put a flame to them.

If one day, miraculously, this poem is translated and you recognise
yourself in it, don't call the publishers to ask for me. We won't have
strength and dreams to sing anymore, and anyone to kiss healed lips.

What better than a memory, as when the trees had winter and
birds, and even a future outside Kew Gardens.

MERCEDES CEBRIÁN
(Madrid, 1971)

TERRITORIO MOQUETA

14 Ladbroke Terrace,
London W11 3PG

1)
Decidí enmoquetar
porque mi idea era asentarme allí.
No se enmoqueta para un fin de semana, la moqueta
es irreversible. De la moqueta
no te puedes ir: es fuente de electricidad
estática y lo estático tiene que ver con garrapatas,
con sanguijuelas, con todo lo que se niega
a abandonar la piel—
solo nuestra intervención
logra arrancarlas.
Las ventosas, al menos,
permiten que corra algo de aire entre
ellas y nosotros.

2)
Un caramelo chupado,
un clip, una goma elástica pasada: todo eso
vive en la moqueta o entre la moqueta.
Estaba ahí remetido: no brillaba el clip
ni se dejaba ver el tornasol
del caramelo de menta, ni por asomo destacaba
la goma elástica formando un dibujo sobre el suelo.
Se agazapan las cosas
dentro de la moqueta y hay que aprender
a verlas.

3)
Los Waley-Cohen llevan un tiempo fuera: en su buzón
se amontonan las cartas. Están suscritos a *The Economist*.

MERCEDES CEBRIÁN

CARPETLAND

14 Ladbroke Terrace,
London W11 3PG

1)
I decided to carpet because I planned
to stay. You don't lay a carpet
for Christmas, carpeting
is final. Carpet sticks:
it produces static
and static is like
a tick or a leech, like anything that clings
persistently to
the skin –
and may need surgical
intervention. With cupping at least
some air
circulates.

2)
A sucked sweet,
a hair-grip, a floppy
rubber-band: all this
is living in the carpet, in its pile.
Deep within: no sign
on the floor of
the shine of the grip, the sheen of the mint,
and no trace whatsoever
of the loop of the rubber-band.
Things burrow
inside the carpet, and you must train your eye
to find them.

3)
The Waley-Cohens have been away for weeks: letters
 are stacking up in their mail-box: They subscribe to *The Economist*.

Cuando vuelven a casa se oyen sus pisadas
por encima de mí.
La moqueta amortigua: su pelea de ayer
parecía una declaración de amor.

4)
Hace cuánto que no enarbolo la bandera
del aquí estoy yo, hace cuánto
que los pies no afirman: «Debajo de nosotros
hay un campo magnético». Clavar
la bandera estadounidense sobre la moqueta o escoger
una pica con una gran cruz de Calatrava en medio
(cuidado, niños: viene el Duque de Alba con su calzado
del siglo dieciséis y os dejará manchada
de barro la moqueta).

5)
Ocurrió la catástrofe: unas manchas
de chorizo en la moqueta *beige*
la afean para siempre —aquí mi pan y yo
nos caímos del bocadillo que fuimos una vez, dice el rastro
aceitoso. Pues bienaventurado el embutido graso porque él
sí logra dejar huella.

6)
Lo más cercano a una adolescente
lo soy en la moqueta. Un encierro
de horas en mi cuarto
con las piernas en sitios infrecuentes, una caja
con una llavecita que esconde mis tesoros.
La moqueta es testigo
y es cómplice a la vez. Al igual que la sangre
no debería verse (cuando sale a la luz
se considera herida o hemorragia), la moqueta
no nos muestra sus calvas.
¿Había dicho ya que la moqueta esconde?

They're back now. I can hear their footsteps
overhead.
Carpet muffles things. Their quarrel last night
could have been billing and cooing.

4)
It's ages since we flew the flag of here I am,
ages since our feet declared: below us lies
a magnetic field. To thrust the Stars
and Stripes into the carpet, or to choose
a banner with a great big Calatrava cross
(look out kiddies: here comes the Duke of Alba
in his Sixteenth Century boots and he'll trail mud
all over the carpet).

5)
Disaster has struck: chorizo stains
on the beige carpet. It's ruined forever.
'Here my bread and me
fell out once and for all
of the sandwich we made up together',
so says the splodge.
Well blessed is this greasy sausage,
for it's certainly made its mark.

6)
I'm at my closest to being a teenager
on the carpet. Locked away
in my room for hours, with my legs
at odd angles, and a box
with a little key, with all my treasures in,
with the carpet as witness
and accomplice. Just as blood
should be kept out of sight (in daylight
it's known as wound or haemorrhage),
the carpet won't show us its bare patches.
Didn't I say carpet hides things?

7)
Pero no existe el encima, el sobre la moqueta.
Enmoquetar equivale a tomar la Bastilla. En la moqueta
se está o no se está. La moqueta es radical:
    paladas
de moqueta pueden llegar a cubrirnos
por completo —yo nunca dije
que la moqueta fuese sólida.

7)
Look, there's no such thing as on
or on top of the carpet. Putting down a carpet
is like storming the Bastille.
Carpet is all or nothing: shovelfuls
of carpet can cover us
from head to toe – I never said
carpet was solid.

ÓSCAR CURIESES
(Madrid, 1972)

HOMBRE EN AZUL (fragmentos)

[19 de diciembre]
Recuerdo los paseos solitarios por la orilla del Thames tras
la adolescencia. Era de noche. Lluvia, oscuridad,
podredumbre y un ligero viento. La sangre mezclándose
con algo que no sé definir bien en mi interior. Lo respiraba
todo. En esos vagabundeos yo era una mezcla de Tiziano,
Baudelaire y un chapero *cockney*.

[25 de septiembre]
Aquel garabato de Michael Alvarado sobre la pasarela
del Thames: «Pensar con el cuerpo».

[21 de enero]
Muchos de mis personajes han salido de la pintura
de Velázquez. En su *Coronación de Baco*, los borrachos
son semejantes a los que habitan mis cuadros, solo
que varios siglos después en el Soho de Londres.

[7 de septiembre]
Sobre la violencia de mis cuadros se podrían decir muchas
cosas… Pero esto implicaría no olvidar una serie de hechos y
circunstancias sociales destacables. Recuérdese el conflicto
irlandés y las dos guerras mundiales, las más atroces que
el ser humano ha provocado y recuerda. Y permítanme
subrayar en ese sentido el Blitz: ochenta noches seguidas de
bombardeos sobre Londres por el ejército del Tercer Reich.
La violencia de mi obra en relación a todo lo anterior
resulta infantil, muy poca cosa.

[7 de noviembre]
Solo he podido pintar en Londres, lo demás han sido
tentativas frustradas. Por eso he regresado aquí una vez
tras otra. Niza, Tánger, París… solo me proporcionaron
la distancia necesaria para tomar conciencia de mi

ÓSCAR CURIESES

MAN IN BLUE (*fragments*)

[December 19th]
I remember solitary walks along the Banks of the Thames post adolescence. It was night-time. Rain, dark, decay and a light wind. My blood mingling with something I can't name inside me. I breathed it all in. In those wanderings I was part Titian, part Baudelaire, part cockney tart.

[September 25th]
That Michael Alvarado doodle on the Thames Path: 'Thinking with the body'.

[January 21st]
Many of my people come from Velázquez paintings. In his *Triumph of Bacchus,* the drunks are much like the ones in my pictures, only several centuries later in Soho, London.

[September 7th]
There are a lot of things you could say about the violence in my pictures… But it would be necessary to bear in mind a significant series of facts and lived events. Think of the Irish Troubles and the two World Wars, the most horrific human beings have caused and still remember. And may I single out the Blitz in that regard: London bombed for eighty consecutive nights by the air force of the Third Reich. The violence in my work, compared to all that, is childlike, insignificant.

[November 7th]
I've only ever been able to paint in London, when I tried elsewhere it ended in failure. So again and again I came back here. Nice, Tangiers, Paris… they only provided me with the distance necessary to understand the impossibility

imposibilidad de escapar. Es lo mismo que les sucede
a los personajes de mis cuadros.

[28 de junio]
Estoy seguro de que después de mi muerte gran parte
de mi pintura desaparecerá de Londres e Inglaterra para
entrar en una especie de purgatorio. Los británicos nunca
me han tenido en gran estima… Con todo, no creo que se
pueda borrar la presencia de mi trabajo de algunos museos
y colecciones destacables, ni tampoco el impacto que
produce en quienes se asoman a ella de manera azarosa.
Pero lo más importante, estoy seguro de que la huella
que he dejado en la figuración y en sus detractores
perdurará.

[22 de noviembre]
En los cielos de Londres siempre está Turner. Reaparece
una y otra vez.

[13 de noviembre]
Poco tiempo antes de morir mi amigo Alberto Giacometti
me comentó: «Cuando estoy en Londres, me siento
homosexual». Nunca supe cómo interpretar aquello…

[8 de julio]
Hace muy pocos días sonreí al escuchar lo siguiente:
«El señor Bacon es también una especie de *performer*.
Su estudio de Reece Mews es en sí mismo una obra
descomunal, una *performance* total, ralentizada a lo
largo de casi treinta años de trayectoria».

[27 de julio]
Mi estudio de Reece Mews, como una metáfora de mi
existencia: un gran estercolero del que han salido algunas
obras notables.

of escape. The people in my paintings are experiencing
the same thing.

[June 28th]
I'm sure that when I'm dead much of my art will disappear
from London and England and end up in a sort of purgatory.
The British have never held me in high esteem… Even so,
I don't think the presence of my work can be erased from
a few museums and important collections, nor its impact on
those who come upon it unexpectedly. But chiefly I'm sure
I've made a lasting impression on figurative art and
on its detractors.

[November 22nd]
Turner is ever present in London skies. Again and again he
is there.

[November 13th]
Not long before he died my friend Alberto Giacometti
remarked to me: 'Whenever I'm in London I feel homosexual'.
I never knew what to make of that…

[July 8th]
A few days ago I smiled when I heard this:
'Mr. Bacon is also a kind of *performer*,
His studio in Reece Mews is in itself
a work of art, a total slow-motion *performance*
enacted over almost thirty years'.

[July 27th]
My Reece Mews studio, as a metaphor for my
existence: a shit-hole out of which some great work
has come.

TERESA GUZMÁN
(Don Benito, Badajoz, 1972)

LLEGAR HASTA AQUÍ

Todo este tiempo para llegar hasta ti
aquí y ahora, a la próxima parada
que se anuncia en el vagón de cola
donde no se sabe si todo empieza
o solo se termina. Donde los años
son ya siempre años pasados.
Todo este tiempo convirtiendo la sal en arena.
Curándome los labios de silenciosas palabras
que ni siquiera ahora y aquí
llegaran a su destino.
Viajeros de ida y vuelta
que habitan a diario estos trenes.
Niñas que se maquillan precisamente cuando
no queda tiempo de arreglar el futuro.
Mientras un caballero con rastas en el pelo
cede su sitio a una dama,
que en ese instante se ha sentido mayor
por primera vez en toda su vida.

«—The next station is Whitechapel»,
anuncia una voz de timbre familiar.
Mientras miro por la ventana en busca de árboles
y solo veo el blanco de los azulejos
que abrillantaron las espaldas
que en ellos buscaron el descanso.
Todo este tiempo detenido para llegar aquí,
a una ciudad en la nunca estuviste.

TERESA GUZMÁN

GETTING TO HERE

All this time to get to you
here and now, to the next stop
you hear announced in the guard's van
where you don't know if everything is beginning
or just ending. Where years
are already years gone by.
All this time to turn salt into sand.
Curing my lips with silent words
that even here and now
won't reach their destination.
Season-ticketholders who every day
inhabit these trains.
Girls meticulously fixing their make-up when
no time is left to fix the future.
While a man with dreadlocks
gives his seat to a woman
who in that instant feels old
for the first time in her life.

'The next station is Whitechapel'
announces a familiar-sounding voice.
While I look out of the window to see some trees
and only see the white of tiles
that got their lustre from the backs
of those who rest against them.
All this time stopped to get to here,
to a city where you've never been.

ERNESTO GARCÍA LÓPEZ
(Madrid, 1973)

SOUTH LONDON
(corte arbitrario)

> *Estamos condenados a escribir,*
> *y a dolernos del ocio que conlleva este paseo de hormigas,*
> *esta cosa de nada y para nada tan fatigosa como el álgebra*
> *o el amor frío pero lleno de violencia que se practica en los puertos.*
> ENRIQUE LIHN

lugar hendido
    sin más acecho que un fin:
lugar que ronda el animal de la locura—

en lugares   desafectos
        inventados
algunas criaturas portan el estandarte de la luz
y
dado
que el paisaje se muestra ininteligible
muevo el ánimo
    esparzo la mirada
        desordeno esa realidad distinta—

llevo tiempo callando por la boca
y hablando en el silencio

asido a un pálpito
de *escritura-labranza* que todo lo comprime
    lo desasía
    lo deja en nada:

preguntándome hasta cuándo durará esta *tormenta de mierda*
que anticipara Bolaño

y es presagio
de impedir lo dicho
fuera de su temblor   fantasma

ERNESTO GARCÍA LÓPEZ

SOUTH LONDON
(arbitrary cut)

> *We are condemned to write,*
> *and undergo the pain involved in this procession of ants,*
> *this empty pointless thing, as tedious as algebra*
> *or love grown cold though full of the violence of harbours.*
> ENRIQUE LIHN

place rent in two
    with no more ambush than an aim:
place where the beast of madness prowls –

in inimical   invented
       places
some creatures bear the standard of the light
and
since
the landscape seems incomprehensible
I *stir* my soul
    scatter my attention
        disorder this otherness –

for a while I have sealed my lips
and spoken in silence

held to a heartbeat
of *writing-yeomanry* that crushes everything
        undoes it
    reduces it to nothing:

wondering how long this *shit-storm*
foretold by Bolaño will last

an it's an omen
to impede speech
beyond its vibration   ghost

                turista ciego
                caricia anunciadora de su propia inquietud
Lambeth es una orilla y su secuencia
sonido contra el mundo de la memoria

zorro reventado
sobre los fangos

un lugar (quizá) donde caza este poema

      *

y en el origen:

parentesco
descendencia
filiación

naturaleza empujada   a las arenas

ríos de antílopes muertos

puntadas de habla
trocitos de ojo
aluvión de historias   junto a las prohibiciones los incestos los
matrimonios:

entregarse a la imposible antropología y velarla
      luego aquella materia
del *hacia-dentro* sorbiendo su locura como un viejo la sopa—

en el principio fueron la alianza y la rapiña:
mujeres secuestradas para asociar la especie
mujeres hoy que pugnan por liberarse en las calles de Brixton
en los mercados de Brixton
en los respiraderos de Brixton

en el principio fueron los desiertos pelados
el eco desvaído
un lobo entre alamedas

                    blind tourist
                    caress foreseeing its own disquiet
Lambeth is a shore and a sequence
a sound against the world of memory

a burst fox
on the mud-banks

a hunting-ground (perhaps) for this poem

   *

and at the origin:

parentage
descent
affiliation

nature propelled   to the sands

rivers of dead antelopes

stitches of speech
little bits of eye
torrents of stories   with prohibitions incest
marriages:

surrender oneself to the impossible anthropology and guard it
          then that matter
of *inwardness* slurping its madness like a old man his soup –

in the beginning were alliance and rapine:
women kidnapped to form the species
women today who fight for their liberation in the Brixton streets
in Brixton Market
in the vents of Brixton

in the beginning were treeless deserts
the feeble echo
a wolf in poplar groves

y como otra alimaña más
        (atizadora en su nerviosismo)
el hombre repite este mismo balbuceo

    *

ya no pienso
        dejo descargar la voladura
ante
un
        habitar que multiplica su ignorancia
        en la ciudad del mercadeo y los cadáveres infinitos

ninguna pastilla
asume el aguante por lo increado:

fallo del sistema

corte arbitrario

      casi nada se aviene a razones
simplemente
      dispara   propulsa   proyecta
su *sinsaber*
contra una superficie de Vauxhall

entonces comprendo que lo oculto refluye inútilmente hacia nosotros
y que sucede dentro de la red secreta
donde se desordena y reordena la misma inutilidad—

viene entonces el devenir
              la deriva:

                  Kennington / Oval / West Norwood / Balham…

hay que planificar la temperatura de la sala para que nuestros trabajadores intermitentes sigan cumpliendo su función

estamos en guerra, darling

and like one more vermin
        (rousing in his nerviness)
the man goes on with his stammering

*

I don't think any more
        I fire up the explosion
in
the face of
        an inhabiting multiplying its ignorance
        in the city of hustlers and infinite corpses

no pill
assumes patience for the uncreated

systemic error

arbitrary cut

    almost nothing agrees to talks
it just
    shoots   propels   projects
its *notknowing*
against a Vauxhall wall

then I understand that the hidden flows back in vain to us
and that this happens within a secret network
where the same vanity is dismantled and restored –

then comes the development
        the drift:

        Kennington / Oval / West Norwood /Balham…

we have to plan the temperature of the hall so our temporary staff continue to do their work

we're at war, darling

la guerra-niña
de los instrumentos y la economía

huelgas hermosas como madrugadas
madrugadas hermosas como huelgas

                Kennington / Oval / West Norwood / Balham...

arden las tiendas inventadas en los puertos
se transforman en   c
                              ó
                              l
                              e
                              r
                              a
                              d
                              e
                              o
                              s
                              c
                              u
                              r
                              i
                              d
                              a
                              d

       *

para afrontar la vertiginosa
la crucificada
la que sigue evitando el chasquido torpe
la perfecta y tristemente reconocida
la nigromante y sempiterna
                    ala de grisura
esta ciudad se olvida de cuanto ha mentido en la historia
pero qué ciudad no ha mentido en la historia...

quizá por eso su cuerpo
se acorta hasta parecer limadura deforme

the girl-war
of instruments and the economy

strikes as beautiful as dawns
dawns as beautiful as strikes

                        Kennington / Oval / West Norwood /Balham…

invented stores burn in the docks
they are transformed into   a
                                  n
                                  g
                                  e
                                  r
                                  o
                                  f
                                  d
                                  a
                                  r
                                  k
                                  n
                                  e
                                  s
                                  s

    *

to confront the dizzying
the crucified
the continually avoiding the clumsy click
the perfect and sadly recognised
the necromancing, sempiternal
                            wing of greyness
this city forgets how much it has lied through history
but what city hasn't lied through history…

maybe that's why its body
shrinks till it looks like misshapen shavings

1989
1992   2001
                       2002
                       2003
la raya inacabada
las bombas lejos
                       2005 y la city
                       2006 y el recorte de la dicha
                       2007 y otra vez el vendaval
                       2008 en el húmero
                       2009 señalando con su dedo
la *salida-mancha* de los hombres de New Cross

: alguna tarde
bajo otra armadura celeste
tendremos que decirnos la verdad
como si fuera un invernadero de sombras

*

hiato   suspendido en hiato
roto el vínculo del lenguaje
fr   a
            gmen
ta   do
en los despachos de *University College London*

se mezclan los recuerdos
se alteran los recuerdos
se *samplean* las grabaciones anteriores a los recuerdos:

Jamaica es un zarpazo de Camberwell
Camberwell un pozo ciego de Peckham
Peckham otra penumbra de Stockwell

fragmentaciones reunidas en el autobús
que escupe tiempo y espacio—

1989
1992   2001
                       2002
                       2003
the uncompleted line
the bombs now far away
                       2005 and the city
                       2006 and the cut of luck
                       2007 and the gales are back
                       2008 in the flue
                       2009 the pointing finger
the *departure-stain* of the men of New Cross

: one afternoon
beneath another celestial armour
we'll have to tell ourselves the truth
as if it were a greenhouse of shadows

*

hiatus   suspended in hiatus
broken the link of language
fr   a
         gme
nt   ed
in the offices of *University College London*

memories mingle
memories alter
recordings made before the memories are *sampled*

Jamaica is a whack from Camberwell
Camberwell is a blind well of Peckham
Peckham another penumbra of Stockwell

breakages collected in the bus
spitting time and space –

si gané esta costa fue por la ligadura
profunda
que une los dos lados del dolor:

puertos de un dólar
de una libra
de un euro

ríos de antílopes muertos
ríos de plástico muerto
ríos por donde atravesar el estallido

Londres, 2009–2018

if I came to this coast it was because of
the deep bond
between both sides of pain:

single dollar harbours
pound harbours
euro harbours

rivers of dead antelopes
rivers of dead plastic
rivers on which to navigate the explosion

London, 2009-2018

ANTONIO RESECO
(Villanueva de la Serena, Badajoz, 1973)

TRAFALGAR SQUARE

Desde lo alto de su columna,
Nelson sospecha que el mundo,
esa esfera que guarda los licores
con puntualidad y sin secretos,
se ha vuelto demasiado grande.
De la Antártida hasta el Norte
se trazan incontables meridianos.

El astrolabio ya no revela
una nomenclatura para las estrellas
y, bajo las aguas, apenas sobra
espacio para un lobo del océano.
Los viajes son ahora más que nunca
la diversión de los pobres.

Un constante trasiego de personas
recuerda que incluso el inglés,
la lengua franca del planeta Tierra,
soporta con dificultad tanto mestizaje.
Pero es obvio que desde un otero
no se aprecian los pequeños detalles.

El catalejo, que todo lo contempla,
es un avance diminuto para una humanidad
que cuenta sus distancias en gigas.
Para comprender la existencia
no basta con la observación:
es preciso vivirla.

Desde lo alto, se ve a los barcos
fondear entre el gentío del sábado
que aprovecha las horas de sol
para solazarse ante los monumentos públicos.
En cambio, a bordo de un galeón

ANTONIO RESECO

TRAFALGAR SQUARE

From up there on his column,
Nelson suspects that the world,
that sphere that holds the liquids in
so carefully, so openly,
has become too wide.
From Antarctica towards the North
countless meridians are drawn.

The astrolabe no longer features
the names of all the stars
and, undersea, there's barely
room for the seals.
More than ever now, the poor
love to travel.

The constant to-and-fro of people
reminds that even English,
the lingua franca of planet Earth,
can hardly cope with so many borrowings.
But clearly from an eminence
one can't appreciate the finer points.

The all-seeing spyglass
is a tiny step forward for a mankind
counting its distances in gigas.
Observation can't suffice
to understand an existence:
life must be lived.

From up there you can see the ships
anchor among the Saturday crowds
taking advantages of the sunshine
to bask before the public monuments.
But, on board a galleon

no hay civilización, ni pasado ni futuro,
no hay explicación para el tráfico de aviones
que tatúan siluetas de lana mortecina
sobre la estratosférica epidermis del progreso.

Sin duda, resulta pavoroso pensar
que el corazón del Imperio
sirve apenas para celebrar las victorias
de algún equipo de rugby o de la selección inglesa,
o para echar de comer a las palomas
en puro ejercicio de descargo:
Occidente duerme así más tranquilo.

En la madurez del Almirante
la ecuación del orden resolvía su incógnita
con la obediencia. Ahora
la mutación ha alcanzado a los isleños:
algunos duermen la siesta;
otros cenan demasiado tarde.

El tiempo pasa. Incluso para los inmortales.
El tiempo es un horror que escucha
el gemido de lo efímero sin clemencia.
Nadie quiere pertenecer a una empresa
que no proporcione ciertas dosis de estabilidad.

Desde lo alto de su pedestal
el Almirante Nelson asume
que los diseños cartográficos
ya no conducen hasta los confines del mundo,
sino más bien al contrario.
Es el mundo el que se conduce
hasta el basamento de su columna,
donde cuatro mansos leones
interpretan el verdadero sentido
de la jungla.

there is no civilization, or past or future,
there is no explanation for the air-traffic
tattooing silhouettes of fading wool
into the stratospheric epidermis of progress.

No doubt it's startling to realise
the centre of the Empire
only serves to celebrate the victories
of a rugby team or the England squad
or for feeding the pigeons,
only for proclamation of innocence:
So the West sleeps more peacefully.

In the Admiral's prime
the equation of order solved its enigma
in obedience. Now
change has overtaken the islanders:
some take a siesta;
others dine absurdly late.

Time goes by. Even for the immortals.
Time is a terror; it hears
mercilessly the moan of the ephemeral.
Nobody wants to belong to an enterprise
that can't provide a measure of stability.

From up there on his pedestal
Admiral Nelson accepts
that cartography no longer
travels to the edges of the world
but rather the opposite.
The world travels
to the base of his column,
where four tame lions
stand for the real significance
of the jungle.

JOSÉ LUIS REY
(Puente Genil, Córdoba, 1973)

MILAGRO EN LONDRES

El milagro es tan solo el gong del mundo.
Levanta pájaros, nubes.
Y pronuncia palacios y poemas.
La túnica del monje llevaba cascabeles.
En Picadilly Circus le ofrecieron ginebra.
Pero él vio las luces y prefirió seguir adelante.
Y vagaba perdido por un sueño
o por una ciudad. (A veces son lo mismo).
Pocos oyen la luz, pero la luz
se desliza cantando entre los hombres.
Era una noche fría. Oxford Street
era un barco pirata encallado en la niebla.
Y había diamantes en el cofre del viento.
Y en una noche alegre puede el hombre
crear su reino de esperanza azul.
Como la chispa al fin brota el poema.
Y nace de lo oscuro, con un afán de luz.
Era una noche fría, ya lo he dicho.
Y pocos vieron deslizarse al monje,
subir entre las nubes panaderas,
sumergirse cantando en otro aire.
Ya había agujas de hielo en las ventanas
y góndolas en Hyde Park. Y jirafas
paseando tranquilas por la City.
Sentiremos cariño al recordarlo.
Una muchacha de ojos grises nos guio hasta el puente.
En las aguas oscuras vi una rosa.
El río quería ahogarla, poseerla.
Y al oír cascabeles la flor se fue elevando
como una palabra en la luz tibia,
como una verdad en el poema.
Y la rosa y el monje se perdieron
por el aire más alto. Y ya tan solo
sentíamos dolor. Pero la muerte

JOSÉ LUIS REY

MIRACLE IN LONDON

Miracle is only the gong of the world.
It scatters birds and clouds.
And declares palaces and poems.
There were little bells on the monk's robes.
In Piccadilly Circus they offered him gin.
But he saw the lights and moved on.
And he wandered lost in a dream
or in a city. (Sometimes there's no difference.)
Few men hear light, but the light
sings as it slips between men.
It was a cold night. Oxford Street
was a pirate ship muffled in the fog.
and there were diamonds in the treasure-chest of the wind.
And on a joyful night man may
build an empire from blue hope.
At last the poem flowers like a spark.
Is born from the dark, with a wish for light.
It was a cold night, as I said.
And few saw the monk slip away,
rise through the floury clouds,
submerge himself in song in other airs.
Now there were ice-needles on the windows
and gondolas in Hyde Park. And giraffes
strolling through the City.
We'll feel warm at the memory of it.
A girl with grey eyes led us to the bridge.
In the dark waters I saw a rose.
The river tried to swallow it, possess it.
And when it heard the little bells the flower arose
like a word in the tepid light,
like a truth in the poem.
And the monk and the rose disappeared
in the heights of the air. And now
all we felt was pain. But death

engaña a los que aún viven en sombras.
A veces aún oímos cascabeles.
Y sentimos cariño al recordarlo.
Yo vi a Juan de la Cruz caminando por Londres una noche muy fría,
con mi hermano y amigos junto al río.
Y Juan del aire entero y la alegría.
Y vi la maravilla permanente,
vi la rosa inmortal, la rosa única.
Vi la vida brillar. Porque el milagro
es la luz que regala la belleza.

tricks those who live in the shadows.
Sometimes we still hear little bells.
And we feel warm at the memory.
I saw John of the Cross walking through London on a very cold night,
with my brother and some friends by the river.
And John of the whole air and of joy.
And I saw unceasing wonder,
I saw the immortal, the only rose.
I saw life shine. For the miracle
is beauty's gift of light.

IGNACIO CARTAGENA
(Alicante, 1977)

HEATHROW

No hicieron otra cosa que abrazarse en todo el viaje.
Las teníamos detrás de nuestro asiento.

—X nos espera a la salida —decía una
en cirílico a la otra. Y tú: «Son casi niñas:
espero que al tal *equis* lo detenga la Interpol».

Pidieron una copa, y luego otra
—licor blanco, sin mezclas, mucho hielo—.

Confieso que soñé, por un momento,
con rayos de cerveza sin filtrar entre las nubes.

Volaba nuestro avión a lo que queda de una isla.

IGNACIO CARTAGENA

HEATHROW

The girls spent the whole flight clinging to one other.
They were in the seat behind us.

'X is waiting for us in Arrivals' one of them said
in Cyrillic to the other. And you said 'They're no more than children:
I hope this X gets nabbed by Interpol'.

They ordered a drink, then a second –
white rum, no mixer, plenty of ice –

I confess I dreamt, for a moment,
of rays of unfiltered beer between the clouds.

Our plane was flying to the remnant of an island.

JOSÉ MANUEL DÍEZ
(Zafra, Badajoz, 1978)

ANÓNIMO LONDINENSE

Un hombre como tantos, indefenso.
Lo conocí bebiendo en una esquina
de un callejón de Londres,
murmurando improperios a la gente, cantando
cierta canción inglesa sin sentido
para un inglés, mas sí para un borracho.
Pugnaba contra un joven
cuatro veces más sobrio y corpulento,
lo vi encajar más golpes
de los que nadie debe recibir en su vida.
Se enmarañaba el gusto de la sangre
con el dulzor del vino en su garganta.
Sonreía y gritaba:
Let's put the X in Sex!

Un hombre como tantos, de mirada salvaje,
desdentado, barbudo, con un par de zapatos
y una libra esterlina en el bolsillo
de una vieja chaqueta sin botones.
Un hombre, un hombre, un hombre,
de los muchos perdidos.
Evitaba farolas, balcones entreabiertos,
muchachas sonrientes.
Debía algún dinero en todas partes.
Planeaba una muerte silenciosa y cercana.

Un hombre, un simple hombre.
Solitario y hermoso.
Derrotado y con vida.

JOSÉ MANUEL DÍEZ

ANONYMOUS LONDONER

A man like so many others, helpless.
I found him drinking on an alley corner
in London,
muttering obscenities at people, singing
an English song meaningless
for an Englishman, but full of meaning for a drunk.
He was fighting a young man
four times his size and four times soberer,
I saw him take more punches
than anyone should in a whole lifetime.
The taste of blood
mingled with the sweet wine in his throat.
He had a smile on his face and he caterwauled:
Let's put the X in Sex!

A man like so many others, with a wild look,
no teeth, a beard, a pair of shoes,
and a pound in the pocket
of his buttonless jacket.
A man, a man, a man
of the numberless lost.
Who avoided street-lamps, half-open balconies,
smiling girls.
Who owed money everywhere.
Who was planning on dying quietly, soon.

A man, no more.
Lonely and beautiful.
Defeated, alive.

JOSÉ DANIEL GARCÍA
(Córdoba, 1979)

ABISINIA ERA EL BLANCO, YA NO

Entré en la web de *Harrods*,
encargué una escafandra
serigrafiada
con palabras y ejemplos
de un diccionario escolar
monolingüe
          y me sumergí,
buceando a pulmón,
en los caladeros de la lengua inglesa;
también en sus acuíferos
y en sus ríos
atestados de *slang*.

Endurecí mis brazos echando redes
sobre preposiciones y perífrasis;
para los verbos irregulares,
caña de pesca y cebo
              de tres días.

Los fonemas fueron capturados
con técnicas de arrastre
en embarcaciones diminutas.

Pero la prosodia es un arte difícil.

¿Atrapar un acento sin arpón
y una pipa entre los labios?
Improbable.

JOSÉ DANIEL GARCÍA

ABYSSINIA WAS THE GOAL, NO LONGER

I clicked on *Harrods* website,
ordered a diving-suit
screen-printed
with words and examples
from a monolingual
compact dictionary
     and I went
snorkelling
in the deep waters of English;
into its aquifers too
and its rivers
rich in slang.

I built up my arm-muscles netting
prepositions and compound verbs;
for irregular verbs I used
a rod and three-day-old
     bait.

The phonemes were caught
by drag-fishing
in a tiny boat.

But prosody is a difficult art.

Capturing an accent with no harpoon
and a pipe between your lips?
I don't think so.

MARIO MARTÍN GIJÓN
(Villanueva de la Serena, Badajoz, 1979)

LONDRES 2007

Liverpool Street

ca*fé*
    de las hor
           migas
que seguir
      o te empujan

(*you stand in my way, what did you expect?*)

más tarde ardí(ll)as
             en el parque

hasta la Victoria
        Station

British Muse
      um
          anidad
di
  sé(ccio)nada

Cleopatra (mo)mía
              unacted desires

MARIO MARTÍN GIJÓN

LONDON 2007

Liverpool Street

coffee
    army of ants/crumbs

you follow
    or they shove you aside

(you stand in my way, what do you expect?)

later the squirrels (you shining)
                                in the park

on to Victory/ia
        Station

British Muse-
      (h)um
           -anity
dissected/I know nothing

Cleopatra (mum)my
            unacted desires

JÈSSICA PUJOL
(Barcelona, 1982)

RIVER WALK

to Elizabeth Guthrie

We believed it	was a good thing
that you decided	to keep still
Good that there were	tall architectures
conglomerates of crystals	and a river walk
Because meanwhile	we don't believe
you got a flat	with views
to Brompton's crosses	God turned into
an irritated	sigh
and park trees	hid cat's grins
Where time passes	and ferns
I also	settled
We believed	love
was in our thought	the river
water	tweets in cages
ALL	nature's plots
But	I still swim
with your image	in easy metaphors
you don't know	how the lie
crawls	
	Tides and boredom
across the sewage	from my toilet
towards you	like Angel Falls
my writing	a parachuted Altazor
But you don't know	the sigh
when I wake up	from sand

and your arms   are rolling
in a microscopic   dew drop
in a dried bit of sleep   I wash

MARÍA SALVADOR
(Granada, 1986)

LOS INVERTEBRADOS DE HAMMERSMITH

And God, I know I'm one.
The House of the Rising Sun

Insectos trepan por los muros de nuestra casa. Ascienden rápidos e imposibles, encontrando cada espacio abierto, destruyendo el aislamiento, saltando al vacío. A veces escuchamos los gritos del viento, y es entonces cuando las multitudes se agolpan hacia nosotros —tendremos que matarlos, por supuesto, pero eso no impedirá que más insectos se reproduzcan en nuestros muros—. *Al menos no son cucarachas*, le digo al hombre al que quiero, mientras recojo con papel una cochinilla. Se encoge y rueda por la moqueta, pero la perseguimos sin piedad hasta mandarla a *un lugar mejor*. Centenares de insectos llaman a nuestros cristales, que empiezan a quebrarse con la lluvia intensa de primeros de mes. Trepan las escaleras del edificio, acechan nuestra puerta —estamos rodeados por los invertebrados, esos inocentes que desean nuestro calor, la protección que solo a nosotros nos pertenece.

MARÍA SALVADOR

THE HAMMERSMITH INVERTEBRATES

And God, I know I'm one.
THE HOUSE OF THE RISING SUN

Insects climb the walls of our house. Up they go quick and impossible, seeking out each open space, abolishing separateness, leaping into the void. Sometimes we hear the cries of the wind, and that is when the multitudes descend on us – we'll have to kill them, of course, but that won't stop more insects multiplying on our walls –. *At least they aren't cockroaches,* I say to the man I love, scooping up a woodlouse with a piece of paper. It curls up and rolls over the carpet, but we hunt it down showing no mercy and send it to *a better place*. Hundreds of insects knock on our windows, which are starting to give way under the heavy rain of the beginning of the month. They climb the stairs of the building, lay siege to our front door – we are ringed by invertebrates, those innocents who yearn for our warmth, the shelter that belongs to us alone.

SOURCES OF THE POEMS

FRANCISCO MARTÍNEZ DE LA ROSA: *Obras literarias de D. Francisco Martínez de la Rosa* [*Literary Works by Mr. Francisco Martínez de la Rosa*], vol. VI, Imprenta de Samuel Bagster, 1838.
DOMINGO MARÍA RUIZ DE LA VEGA: *Recuerdos de la juventud* [*Memories of Youth*], Imprenta de J. Antonio García, 1871.
JOSÉ DE ESPRONCEDA: *Poesías líricas y fragmentos épicos* [*Lyrical Poems and Fragments of Epic*], Castalia, 1989.
JOSÉ ALCALÁ GALIANO: *Estereoscopio social. Colección de cuadros contemporáneos fotografías, acuarelas, dibujos, estampas, caricaturas, grupos, bustos, agua-fuertes, bocetos, vistas, paisajes, bodegones, camafeos, etc., etc., tomados del natural y puestos en verso satírico-humorístico* [*Social Stereoscope. Collection of Contemporary Paintings, Photographs, Watercolours, Sketches, Prints, Cartoons, Groups, Busts, Etchings, Outlines, Views, Landscapes, Still Lives, Cameos, etc., etc., Taken from Nature and Put into Satirical-comical Verse*], Imprenta de José Noguera, 1872.
MIGUEL DE UNAMUNO: *Obras completas* [*Complete Works*], vol. VI, Poesía, Escelicer, 1966.
JOSÉ ANTONIO BALBONTÍN: *A la orilla del Támesis (Poemas del destierro)* [*On the Banks of the Thames (Poems of Exile)*], Ayuntamiento de Santa María de Cayón, 2005.
LUIS CERNUDA: *Las nubes. Desolación de la Quimera* [*Clouds. Desolate Vision*], Cátedra, 1991.
LUIS GABRIEL PORTILLO: *Ruiseñor del destierro* [*Nightingale of Exile*], Anthropos, 1989.
BASILIO FERNÁNDEZ: *Poemas 1927-1987* [*Poems 1927-1987*], Llibros del Pexe, 1991
PEDRO BASTERRA (JOSÉ GARCÍA PRADAS): *La corona de Elizabeth II. Cantos de Pedro Basterra* [*Elizabeth's Crown. Pedro Basterra's Cantos*], author's edition, undated.
JOSÉ MARÍA AGUIRRE RUIZ: *Londres (Ensayo sobre un cierto tiempo)* [*London (an Essay on a Moment in Time)*], Publicaciones Porvivir Independiente, 1980.
MANUEL PADORNO: *Obras completas* [*Complete Works*], vol. I, Pre-Textos, 2016.
RAFAEL GUILLÉN: *Obras completas* [*Complete Works*], vol. II, Almed, 2010.
CARLOS SAHAGÚN: *Primer y último oficio* [*First and Last Offices*], Los Libros de la Frontera, 1981.
JUAN ANTONIO MASOLIVER RÓDENAS: *Poesía reunida* [*Collected Poems*], Acantilado, 1999.
JUAN LUIS PANERO: *A través del tiempo* [*Through Time*], Cultura Hispánica, 1968.

PERE GIMFERRER: *Arde el mar* [*The Sea Is Burning*], Amelia Romero, 1966.
GUILLERMO CARNERO: *Verano inglés* [*English Summer*], Tusquets, 1999.
LEOPOLDO MARÍA PANERO: *Teoría* [*Theory*], 1973; taken from *Poesía 1970-1985* [*Poetry 1970-1985*], Visor, 1993.
RAFAEL ARGULLOL: *Poema* [*Poem*], Acantilado, 2017.
EFI CUBERO: *Revistart*, 2018.
JOAQUÍN SABINA: http://www.poetasandaluces.com/poema/1133/; *Interviú*, March 24th, 2008.
LUIS SUÑÉN: *Vida de poeta* [*The Poet's Life*], Ave del Paraíso, 1998.
ÁNGELES MORA: *Ficciones para una autobiografía* [*Fictions for an Autobiography*], Bartleby, 2015.
JAVIER VIRIATO: *Poemas de Londres* [*London Poems*], STI, 2008. (London Poems *was written between April and November 1976 in the attic of 10 Wandsworth Bridge Road on the edge of Fulham and Chelsea*).
JAVIER PÉREZ WALIAS: *Heterónima*, 4, Spring 2018.
CARLOS MARZAL: *Los países nocturnos* [*Nightlands*], Tusquets, 1996.
EDUARDO MOGA: *Muerte y amapolas en Alexandra Avenue* [*Death and Poppies in Alexandra Avenue*], Vaso Roto, 2017.
MANUEL VILAS: *Amor. Poesía reunida 1988-2010* [*Love. Collected Poems 1988-2010*], Visor, 2010.
JUAN CARLOS MARSET: *Laberinto* [*Labyrinth*], Sibila y Fundación BBVA, 2013.
ANTONIO RIVERO TARAVILLO: *Lo que importa* [*What Matters*], Renacimiento, 2015.
BALBINA PRIOR: *En los andenes de la era Heisei* [*On the Walkways of the Heisei Period*], A la Luz del Candil, 2001.
JAVIER SÁNCHEZ MENÉNDEZ: *Mediodía en Kensington Park* [*Midday in Kensington Gardens*], La Isla de Siltolá, 2015.
MELCHOR LÓPEZ: «Cuaderno inglés (1996)» [*English Notebook (1996)*], en *Según la luz* [*According to the Light*], Trea, 2018.
ANTONIO ORIHUELA: *Esperar sentado* [*Waiting Sitting Down*], La Baragaña, 2012.
JUAN LUIS CALBARRO: *Luke*, nº 185, September-October 2018: http://www.espacioluke.com.
JUAN CARLOS ELIJAS: *Seis sextetos* [*Six Sestets*], La Isla de Siltolá, 2017.
SUSANA MEDINA: *Quimera*, nº 418, October 2018.
DAVID TORRES: *Londres* [*London*], Calima, 2003.
JORDI DOCE: *Campo abierto. Antología del poema en prosa en España (1990-2005)* [*Open Field. Anthology of the Prose Poem in Spain (1990-2005)*], DVD ediciones, 2005.
ANXO CARRACEDO: *La tarde libre* [*The Free Evening*], Ediciones en Huida, 2018.
FRANCISCO LEÓN: *Tiempo entero* [*Time Entire*], Calima, 2002.

JULIO MAS ALCARAZ: *12+1. Una antología de poetas madrileños* [*12+1 Madrid Poets*], Endymion Poesía, 2012.
MERCEDES CEBRIÁN: *Malgastar* [*Squandering*], La Bella Varsovia, 2016.
ÓSCAR CURIESES: *Hombre en azul* [*Man in Blue*], JekyllandJill, 2014. (Man in Blue *features some diaries that the painter Francis Bacon could have written between October 1989 and March 1992*).
TERESA GUZMÁN: *Zapatos para pisar la lluvia* [*Shoes to Tread the Rain*], La Isla de Siltolá, 2016.
ERNESTO GARCÍA LÓPEZ: *Ritual*, Amargord, 2009.
ANTONIO RESECO: *London bureau*, De la luna libros, 2012.
JOSÉ LUIS REY: *La luz y la palabra* [*Light and the Word*], Visor, 2001.
IGNACIO CARTAGENA: *El ocio que nos queda* [*What Remains of Our Leisure*], Sial, 2016.
JOSÉ MANUEL DÍEZ: *El país de los imbéciles* [*The Country of Fools*], Hiperión, 2018.
JOSÉ DANIEL GARCÍA: *Noir*, La Isla de Siltolá, 2017.
MARIO MARTÍN GIJÓN: *Transtierros*, December 13th, 2018: https://transtierrosblog.wordpress.com/2018/12/13/londres-2007-mario-martin/.
JÈSSICA PUJOL: *Now Worry*, Department Press, 2012.
MARÍA SALVADOR: *Kokoro*, October 2018: http://www.revistakokoro.com/losinvertebrados.html.

Lightning Source UK Ltd.
Milton Keynes UK
UKHW010632301019
352594UK00001B/244/P